ENERGY OPPORTUNITIES IN SOUTH AMERICA

HEARING

BEFORE THE

SUBCOMMITTEE ON
THE WESTERN HEMISPHERE

OF THE

COMMITTEE ON FOREIGN AFFAIRS
HOUSE OF REPRESENTATIVES

ONE HUNDRED FIFTEENTH CONGRESS

FIRST SESSION

MAY 17, 2017

Serial No. 115–24

Printed for the use of the Committee on Foreign Affairs

Available via the World Wide Web: http://www.foreignaffairs.house.gov/ or http://www.gpo.gov/fdsys/

U.S. GOVERNMENT PUBLISHING OFFICE

25–455PDF WASHINGTON : 2017

For sale by the Superintendent of Documents, U.S. Government Publishing Office
Internet: bookstore.gpo.gov Phone: toll free (866) 512–1800; DC area (202) 512–1800
Fax: (202) 512–2104 Mail: Stop IDCC, Washington, DC 20402–0001

COMMITTEE ON FOREIGN AFFAIRS

EDWARD R. ROYCE, California, *Chairman*

CHRISTOPHER H. SMITH, New Jersey
ILEANA ROS-LEHTINEN, Florida
DANA ROHRABACHER, California
STEVE CHABOT, Ohio
JOE WILSON, South Carolina
MICHAEL T. McCAUL, Texas
TED POE, Texas
DARRELL E. ISSA, California
TOM MARINO, Pennsylvania
JEFF DUNCAN, South Carolina
MO BROOKS, Alabama
PAUL COOK, California
SCOTT PERRY, Pennsylvania
RON DeSANTIS, Florida
MARK MEADOWS, North Carolina
TED S. YOHO, Florida
ADAM KINZINGER, Illinois
LEE M. ZELDIN, New York
DANIEL M. DONOVAN, Jr., New York
F. JAMES SENSENBRENNER, Jr., Wisconsin
ANN WAGNER, Missouri
BRIAN J. MAST, Florida
FRANCIS ROONEY, Florida
BRIAN K. FITZPATRICK, Pennsylvania
THOMAS A. GARRETT, Jr., Virginia

ELIOT L. ENGEL, New York
BRAD SHERMAN, California
GREGORY W. MEEKS, New York
ALBIO SIRES, New Jersey
GERALD E. CONNOLLY, Virginia
THEODORE E. DEUTCH, Florida
KAREN BASS, California
WILLIAM R. KEATING, Massachusetts
DAVID N. CICILLINE, Rhode Island
AMI BERA, California
LOIS FRANKEL, Florida
TULSI GABBARD, Hawaii
JOAQUIN CASTRO, Texas
ROBIN L. KELLY, Illinois
BRENDAN F. BOYLE, Pennsylvania
DINA TITUS, Nevada
NORMA J. TORRES, California
BRADLEY SCOTT SCHNEIDER, Illinois
THOMAS R. SUOZZI, New York
ADRIANO ESPAILLAT, New York
TED LIEU, California

Amy Porter, *Chief of Staff* Thomas Sheehy, *Staff Director*
Jason Steinbaum, *Democratic Staff Director*

Subcommittee on the Western Hemisphere

JEFF DUNCAN, South Carolina, *Chairman*

CHRISTOPHER H. SMITH, New Jersey
ILEANA ROS-LEHTINEN, Florida
MICHAEL T. McCAUL, Texas
MO BROOKS, Alabama
RON DeSANTIS, Florida
TED S. YOHO, Florida
FRANCIS ROONEY, Florida

ALBIO SIRES, New Jersey
JOAQUIN CASTRO, Texas
ROBIN L. KELLY, Illinois
NORMA J. TORRES, California
ADRIANO ESPAILLAT, New York
GREGORY W. MEEKS, New York

CONTENTS

Page

WITNESSES

LETTERS, STATEMENTS, ETC., SUBMITTED FOR THE HEARING

APPENDIX

ENERGY OPPORTUNITIES IN SOUTH AMERICA

WEDNESDAY, MAY 17, 2017

HOUSE OF REPRESENTATIVES,
SUBCOMMITTEE ON THE WESTERN HEMISPHERE,
COMMITTEE ON FOREIGN AFFAIRS,
Washington, DC.

The committee met, pursuant to notice, at 10:00 a.m., in room 2172 Rayburn House Office Building, Hon. Jeff Duncan (chairman of the subcommittee) presiding.

Mr. DUNCAN. Okay, a quorum being present, the subcommittee will come to order. I would like now to recognize myself for an opening statement.

This is the third hearing that we have had on energy in the Americas since I have begun my chairmanship. I am passionate about this topic because I firmly believe that energy is an important key to creating more jobs for the Americans and to helping our hemisphere achieve a better quality of life via electricity coverage, energy production, and benefitting from the resulting economic growth.

In the past, the U.S. supported energy initiatives in the region through investment and the exploration and production of traditional energy resources, providing regulatory and technical guidance and under the Obama administration renewal energy projects. In fact, a congressional delegation led by me and Ranking Member Sires visited an extensive solar energy project in Chile.

Today, I believe that the U.S. could do much more to prioritize hemispheric-wide energy security in our approach to the region. After all, the discovered and reportedly undiscovered energy potential alone is enormous.

South America is home to a vast wealth of natural resources including nearly 20 percent of the world's proven crude oil reserves and 4 percent of proven natural gas reserves. An effective use of such energy resources could result in more people having a higher quality of life through receiving electricity coverage, a higher number of jobs in needy areas, and greater investment from international companies into the communities where they do business. In addition, the energy landscape is diverse. Venezuela has the largest proven oil reserves in the world and the second largest nat- ural gas reserves in the Americas. Significant oil and natural gas production is also occurring in Argentina, Bolivia, Brazil, Colombia, Ecuador, and Peru.

Furthermore, the hemisphere produces the largest amount of hydroelectric power. Brazil is the world's second largest producer of ethanol and third largest liquid fuel producer. And Colombia is the world's fifth largest producer of coal. Chile also has the world's largest lithium reserves and Argentina possesses one of the world's largest potential markets to produce unconventional hydrocarbons. Similarly, Argentina is also the only Latin American country that is producing commercial quantities of oil from shale deposits. According to the U.S. Energy Information Administration in 2015, Argentina was second of 46 countries in terms of its undiscovered shale gas resource potential, and fourth in its undiscovered shale oil potential. Such prospects offer multiple areas for greater partnership with our country, given the U.S. experience with shale and with the U.S. energy technology.

In addition. Brazil's offshore pre-salt basins may be one of the world's largest oil finds, recoverable volumes of oil reported are estimated at over 40 billion barrels. Combined with Brazil's other 18 on-shore basins, Brazil's energy market offers huge promise for the country, the region, and expanding energy ties with the U.S. Likewise, Colombia and Ecuador and Peru also have significant oil and gas production. And Guyana reportedly possesses substantial amounts of oil offshore. This is in addition to what Paraguay hopes to do in the northern part of the country; and to what Chile hopes to do with furthering other energy sources such as solar in their vast sunny areas.

Today's robust energy landscape in South America is made even more compelling for deeper U.S. engagement given recent political shifts in the region. Countries seem to be waking up to the realization that status economic policies simply do not generate the kind of economic growth that they need. A change appears to be underway and countries are now making reforms to advance free market friendly energy policies and attract foreign investment.

Argentina, Bolivia, Brazil, Colombia, and Peru, have all made some effort to improve their respective regulatory structures. Moreover, South America has become a growing market for U.S. oil and natural gas exports. Over the past decade, U.S. petroleum product exports to the region have grown by over 400 percent and last year for the first time ever U.S. exported liquefied natural gas (LNG) to the region. Argentina, Brazil, and Chile were the first three South American countries to become LNG importers.

Furthermore, under U.S. law, the Department of Energy must prioritize exports of U.S. LNG to countries with which we have free trade agreements. This creates additional opportunities for expedited U.S. LNG exports to Colombia and Peru, as well as to the Caribbean.

Although the price of oil may remain low, energy prospects in South America are plenty. At a time when Venezuela continues to grow more unstable, threatening countries that depend on PDVSA for energy security, and as countries in the Middle East and North Africa continue their volatility, it is critical that the United States work with other energy-producing countries in South America to increase our energy security.

The Western Hemisphere has vast energy potential. The U.S. and South America, along with our neighbors in Canada and Mexico, just need to build on those opportunities and create hemispheric-wide energy security effort using our respective countries' strengths.

I will never forget the experience that Ranking Member Sires and I had last year when we visited the binational dam at Itaipu, the world's second largest hydroelectric plant jointly operated by Paraguay and Brazil. The spillways were open and it was an incredible display of hydroelectric power. The region has an amazing opportunity right now with energy and I look forward to what our witnesses will have to share on the subject and with that, I will turn to the ranking member, Albio Sires, for his opening remarks. Mr. SIRES. Well, good morning, everyone. Thank you to our chairman for holding this important hearing and to our witnesses for taking the time to be here with us today.

Today's hearing looks at both the opportunities and challenges toward enhancing our energy cooperation with South America. I believe integrating our energy interests in the region have been ignored for far too long.

Although we often focus on the resources of the Middle East, it is worth noting that there are significant energy resources right here in our hemisphere. South America is home to vast oil and gas reserves and possesses tremendous renewable energy potential. Venezuela is home to 88 percent of the region's proven oil reserves. In regards to nontraditional source of energy, Brazil is the world's second largest producer of ethanol after the United States.

Engaging with the Caribbean is critical, especially with the petro dollars from a crumbling Venezuela are drying up and the entire country is on the verge of collapse. Unfortunately, Maduro and his cronies have squandered the opportunity this could have brought to the Venezuelan people. Every day, we see the situation becoming more dangerous with the Venezuelan people suffering at the hands of Maduro's authoritarian tactics.

That is why I hope this new administration will build on some of the bipartisan initiatives Congress worked on during the last few years. In 2016, Congress passed H.R. 4939, the U.S.-Caribbean Strategic Engagement Act. With the leadership of Ranking Member Engel and Congresswoman Ileana Ros-Lehtinen, this bill mandates that the State Department develop a strategy to support enhanced engagement with the Caribbean region.

Moreover, the growing presence of anti-democratic actors such as Russia and China whose self-interests are counter to the strategic concerns of the U.S. should not be taken lightly. China pledged to increase trade with the region by $500 billion and foreign investment to $250 billion by 2025, seeking to boost their influence in the resource-rich region.

Immediately following the election of President Trump, China released a white paper calling Latin America and the Caribbean a land of vitality and hope. The U.S. cannot fall behind as the Western Hemisphere plays a critical role in our energy security. Our national security requires that energy policy be a central component of our foreign policy. Furthermore, we should build upon and expand our energy diplomacy efforts, mitigate Caribbean dependence on subsidized Venezuelan oil and support the economic growth of the region in ways that are both relevant and practical to the needs of everyday people. No one single project or initiative is a cure-all for our energy security needs and no proposal will satisfy everyone's need or alleviate every doubt, but we must continue to work with our neighbors to develop a beneficial energy policy for the region.

I look forward to hearing from our panel on how we can address these critical issues. Thank you.

Mr. DUNCAN. I want to thank the ranking member and I want to thank the witnesses as well for being here. I look forward to your testimony.

Before we get started, there is a lighting system in front of you. You are given 5 minutes for your opening statements and the lights will change from green to yellow to red. When it gets to yellow, start trying to wrap up. I will be a little lenient with that, but we will try to stay on schedule.

Also, when we finish your testimony, we will recognize ourselves and I will recognize other members for 5 minutes to ask questions. And I ask that we try to stick to that 5-minute rule.

So with that, the bios are in your information provided. I will not read those. I will just introduce the witnesses. We are going to start with Mr. Pinon for 5 minutes. You are recognized. If you will, there is a button that says talk, cut that microphone on until it is red. There you go.

STATEMENT OF MR. JORGE R. PINON, DIRECTOR, LATIN AMERICA AND CARIBBEAN PROGRAM, JACKSON SCHOOL OF GEOSCIENCES, THE UNIVERSITY OF TEXAS AT AUSTIN

Mr. PINON. Thank you. I would like to thank you, Mr. Chairman, and Ranking Member Sires for giving me the opportunity to underscore South America's energy potential and its contribution to a broader energy integration within the Western Hemisphere. My oral comments will be summarized in my written statement.

The Western Hemisphere holds approximately 35 percent of the world's proven oil reserves, 49 percent of the world's undiscovered conventional oil resources, and 38 percent of the world's technically recoverable shale oil resources.

Not as large, but very important and strategic within the regional context are the Western Hemisphere's natural gas reserves representing 10 percent of the world's proven natural gas reserves, but 42 percent of the world's technically recoverable natural gas shale resources.

It is the ability to monetize and produce these natural gas reserves that gives the Western Hemisphere a competitive advantage by being the second largest natural gas producing region in the world, as its Liquefied Natural Gas, LNG, trade demonstrates.

The challenge in Latin America, Mr. Chairman, is not the lack of oil and natural gas resources, but the host countries' onerous contractual and fiscal terms and conditions, regulatory environment, and the lack of political stability and continuity that international oil companies need in order to invest and sustainably monetize and commercialize those resources.

A good example is Venezuela, the world's largest holder of oil reserves surpassing those of Saudi Arabia, but who is unable to develop its potential as its production has declined from a high of over 3 million barrels per day to less than 2 million barrels per day.

It is also important to highlight that these oil and natural gas resources are concentrated in unconventional deposits and frontier areas making its sustainable and economical extraction challenging as advance technology, high capital requirements, and operational know-how are critical for their development.

The region's energy potential is not only in hydrocarbons, as was stated. More than a quarter of primary energy in Latin America today comes from renewables, mainly from hydropower and biofuels. However, all countries in the region are developing other renewable energy sources, such as wind, solar and biomass-based electricity.

I would like to address, Mr. Chairman, the importance of regional energy integration as the cornerstone to the energy security of the United States. Please note that I avoid mentioning the idealized concept of energy independence since I am deeply concerned that the use of the term would lead us to a state of complacency which would prevent us from recognizing external threats and risks to our energy security, a much broader and strategic concept. The United States needs to support the building of infrastructure and logistic assets which would allow us to monetize and commer- cialize the Western Hemisphere's crude oil, natural gas, refined products, and electric power potential.

We should look at the Western Hemisphere as an integrated, interdependent, and self-sufficient energy market which would provide the United States uninterrupted performance of our energy infrastructure and the ability to react quickly to changes in supply-demand disruptions.

Despite a 70 percent increase in domestic crude oil production since 2008, the United States still imports 49 percent of the crude oil it refines. Canada and Mexico constitute approximately half of all U.S. imports with an additional 18 percent coming from South America. In 2016, the United States exported over 5 million barrels of crude oil and refined products of which nearly 50 percent were destined to Latin America.

The U.S. largest fuel customer in the region is Mexico with approximately 33 percent of total U.S. refined product exports to Latin America; followed by Brazil, Colombia and Ecuador. This new regional trade pattern is expected to continue, since declining refining capacity in Latin America makes it unable to meet its growing demand for clean transportation fuels. U.S. Gulf Coast refineries, operating at 90 percent of utilization today, have become the de facto oil refining center for Latin America.

In conclusion, Mr. Chairman, I would like to briefly address the current situation in Venezuela as I believe that U.S. imports of Venezuelan crude oil and the operations of its U.S. refining subsidiary Citgo could be threatened by external and internal events as a result of the political and economic crisis that Venezuela faces today.

The U.S Government should be ready with contingency plans on possible short-term alternatives on how to replace Venezuelan imports until the free market find its own solutions just like it did during the 2003 Venezuelan oil strike. Also, a casualty from the possible collapse of the Venezuelan government is Cuba who depends on Venezuela to meet its oil imports. The island already is beginning to identify and diversify its oil supply sources and it seems that Russia could play the same supplier role as it did during the Cold War period.

Thank you very much, Mr. Chairman, and members of the subcommittee. I look forward in answering any questions that you might have.

[The prepared statement of Mr. Pinon follows:]

United States House of Representatives
Committee on Foreign Affairs
Subcommittee on the Western Hemisphere

Energy Opportunities in South America Hearing
May 17, 2017

Testimony of Jorge R. Piñon
Interim Director, Center for International Energy and Environmental Policy and Director, Latin America and Caribbean Energy Program,
Jackson School of Geosciences,
The University of Texas at Austin

The opinion and analyses herein do not necessarily state or reflect those of The University of Texas at Austin. The University of Texas at Austin is committed to transparency and disclosure of potential conflicts of interests of its researchers. The "Truth in Testimony" disclosure form is attached and meant to be part of the written and oral testimony.

I would like to thank you Mr. Chairman and ranking member Sires for giving me the opportunity to underscore South America's energy potential and its contribution to a broader regional energy integration within the Western Hemisphere.

My oral comments will be summarizing my written statement.

Oil Resources

The Western Hemisphere holds approximately 35 percent of the world's proven oil reserves, 49 percent of the world's undiscovered conventional oil resources and 38 percent of the world's technically recoverable shale oil resources. (USGS)

Natural Gas Resources

The Middle East and Russia are the world's largest holders of proven natural gas reserves with approximately 73% of total share. (EIA)

Not as large; but very important and strategic within the regional context are the Western Hemisphere's natural gas reserves representing 10 percent of the world's proven natural gas reserves and 42 percent of the world's technically recoverable natural gas shale resources. (USGS)

It is the ability to produce and monetize these natural gas reserves that gives the Western Hemisphere a competitive advantage by being the second largest natural gas producing region in the world; as its Liquefied Natural Gas LNG trade demonstrates. (EIA)

The Main Actors

Crude oil and natural gas resources abound in South America; Venezuela, Guyana, and Trinidad and Tobago in Northern South America Caribbean region; Colombia, Peru, Bolivia, and Ecuador within the Andean community; Argentina and Uruguay in the Southern Cone and Brazil.

Challenge

The challenge in Latin America Mr. Chairman is not the lack of oil and natural gas resources but the host countries onerous contractual and fiscal terms and conditions, regulatory environment and the lack of political stability and continuity that international oil companies need in order to invest and sustainably monetize and commercialize those resources.

A good example is Venezuela, the world's largest holder of oil reserves surpassing those of Saudi Arabia; but who is unable to develop its potential as its production has declined from a high of over 3.0 mmbd to less than 2.0 mmbd. (OPEC)

It is also important to highlight that these oil and natural gas resources are concentrated in unconventional deposits and frontier areas making its sustainable and economical extraction challenging as advance technology, high capital requirements and operational knowhow are critical for their development.

Renewables

The region's energy potential is not only in hydrocarbons as more than a quarter of primary energy in Latin America today comes from renewables, mainly from hydropower and biofuels.

However all countries in the region are developing other renewable energy sources, such as wind, solar and biomass-based electricity.

Brazil, Chile and Mexico ranked amongst the top ten global renewable energy markets in terms of investment in 2015.

The United States, Brazil and Argentina produce today about 73% of world's production of Biofuels. (ENI)

Western Hemisphere Energy Integration

I would like to address Mr. Chairman the importance of regional energy integration as the cornerstone to the Energy Security of the United Sates.

Please note that I avoid mentioning the idealized concept of Energy Independence since I am deeply concerned that the use of the term would lead us to a state of complacency which would prevent us from recognizing external threats and risks to our Energy Security, a much broader and strategic concept.

The United States needs to support the building of infrastructure and logistic assets which would allow us to monetize and commercialize the Western

Hemisphere's crude oil, natural gas, refined products and electric power potential.

We should look at the Western Hemisphere as an integrated, interdependent and self-sufficient energy market which would provide the United States uninterrupted performance of our energy infrastructure and the ability to react quickly to changes in supply-demand disruptions.

Despite a 70% increase in domestic crude oil production since 2008 the United States still imports 49% of the crude oil it refines. Canada and Mexico constitute approximately half of all US imports with an additional 18 percent coming from South America. (EIA)

In 2016 the United States exported over 5.0 mmbd of crude oil and refined products of which nearly 50 percent were destined to Latin America. (EIA)

The U.S. largest fuel customer in the region is Mexico with approximately 33% of total U.S. refined product exports to Latin America; followed by Brazil, Colombia and Ecuador. (EIA)

This new regional trade pattern is expected to continue since declining refining capacity in Latin America makes it unable to meet its growing demand for clean transportation fuels.

U.S. Gulf Coast refineries, operating at 90 percent of utilization, have become the de-facto oil refining center for Latin America. (EIA)

Venezuela-Cuba

Mr. Chairman I would like to briefly address the current situation in Venezuela as I believe that U.S. imports of Venezuelan crude oil and the operations of its U.S. refining subsidiary CITGO could be threatened by external and internal events as a result of the political and economic crisis that Venezuela faces today.

The U.S government should be ready with contingency plans on possible short term alternatives on how to replace Venezuelan imports until the free market find its own solutions just like it did during the 2003 Venezuelan oil strike.

Also a casualty from the possible collapse of the Venezuelan government is Cuba who depends on Venezuela to meet its oil imports.

The Island already is beginning to identify and diversify its oil supply sources and it seems that Russia could play the same supplier role as it did during the cold war period.

The result for Cuba could very well be a second "special period", however the economic impact would not be as dire as in 1991-1992; but this time social unrest in our opinion could pose a risk to the political stability of the country.

Thank you very much Mr. Chairman and members of the Subcommittee; I look forward to answering any questions that you might have.

Mr. DUNCAN. Thank you so much. And now, Ms. Viscidi will be recognized for 5 minutes.

STATEMENT OF MS. LISA VISCIDI, DIRECTOR, ENERGY, CLIMATE CHANGE, AND EXTRACTIVE INDUSTRIES PROGRAM, INTER-AMERICAN DIALOGUE

Ms. VISCIDI. Thank you. I would like to thank the committee and subcommittee chairmen and ranking members.

Mr. DUNCAN. Pull that microphone over just a little bit. Thank you.

Ms. VISCIDI. Thank you and I would like to thank the other committee members for the opportunity to be here today.

My testimony will focus on the energy landscape in South America, the importance of U.S. investment in oil and gas, and clean energy in the region, and opportunities for energy policy engagement between the U.S. and South American countries.

South America is an important destination for energy investment due to abundant natural resources, growing markets, and favorable policy frameworks in several countries. The continent holds massive oil and gas reserves, from the Orinoco heavy oil belt in Venezuela to the Vaca Muerta shale play in Argentina. There is also abundant potential for renewable energy including hydro, wind, and solar.

South America has large domestic markets with rapidly growing consumption of oil for transportation and soaring demand for electricity. Many countries have recently become more open to energy investments, enacting market-friendly policies and regulatory reforms to attract private capital and international expertise. For example, administrations in Brazil and Argentina have removed longstanding barriers to investment in the oil and gas sector; and Colombia, looking to maintain current levels of production and reserves despite the drop in prices has revised its investment terms.

Several South American countries also offer strong incentives for renewable investments such as wind and solar auctions, renewable portfolio standards, and favorable financing. Chile joined Brazil as one of the top ten renewable energy markets globally in 2015, almost doubling its share of renewables investment from 2014. And Argentina held its first two renewable energy auctions late last year.

There are, however, exceptions to this generally more favorable investment climate in South America. Venezuela, marred by political upheaval in an economic crisis, has seen a sharp decline in production and investment. Oil output declined by 235,000 barrels per day in the first three quarters of last year. And it will likely drop below 2 million barrels a day by the end of this year.

As a result, countries in Latin America and the Caribbean that have relied on imports of crude oil and refined products from Venezuela, have turned to alternative oil suppliers and replaced oil with natural gas and renewable energy. Exports of Venezuelan oil to key partners like Jamaica, the Dominican Republic, and even Cuba have declined considerably.

U.S. investors and companies are key partners in developing energy resources and supplying markets in South America thanks to the human, technological, and financial resources of rapidly growing oil and renewable energy industries here, as well as proximity to other countries in the hemisphere.

U.S. investment in energy brings multiple benefits to the U.S. and South America. For South American Governments, oil exports to the U.S. market provide a critical source of revenue, and the development of energy resources is an economic driver for prosperity in the region. Investment in renewable energy also brings environmental benefits. South America has the cleanest electricity matrix in the world, although several large cities face severe local air pollution due to heavy traffic and weak fuel efficiency and fuel quality standards. For the United States, energy investment in South America also has the potential to generate investment revenue and employment in the country.

Foreign investment also facilitates energy trade integration between the U.S. and its neighbors in South America. U.S. relies on South America for almost 20 percent of crude oil imports and South America is emerging as a key market for U.S. LNG.

However, U.S. companies are by no means the only players, and if the U.S. cuts energy ties with South America countries, other actors will likely gain influence. China is a leading investor in oil and gas in many countries and is making inroads into hydropower and other renewable energy development. Russia is also increasing its stake in Venezuela's oil industry. Chinese and Russian engagement in the region is driven by geopolitical, as well as commercial interests.

While most U.S. investment in South America's energy sectors has been market-driven, policy has also played a role in promoting energy integration and cross-border investment. U.S. Government initiatives have helped improve investment climates, create commercial opportunities for U.S. companies and facilitate clear and consistent investment rules.

Collaboration on energy issues in turn helps bolster broader economic, political, and security relations with South American countries, many of which serve as key allies for the United States and cooperative on a range of issues from immigration to counter-narcotics.

Therefore, it is important that the U.S. Government engage with Latin America on energy policy issues as part of broader bilateral relations. Strong diplomatic and economic ties, including free trade agreements, are most important and provide the foundation for energy trade and investment between the United States and South America. Within the energy sector I would highlight two areas of potential and important engagement.

In the oil sector, the U.S. should support reforms that enable private investment and continue to engage in regulatory cooperation including for shale development in Argentina and offshore in Brazil and Colombia.

And in clean energy, I think the U.S. should support clean transportation with countries like Colombia, Brazil, Argentina, and Chile, because sustainable transport is a major challenge for these countries, given the large degree of urbanization, rapidly growing transportation needs and air pollution issues.

In conclusion, given the importance of U.S. energy relations with South America and the rest of the hemisphere, it is critical to maintain energy policy engagement with U.S. allies in the region. That concludes my oral testimony. I look forward to the opportunity to respond to any questions or comments you may have.

[The prepared statement of Ms. Viscidi follows:]

Statement of Lisa Viscidi
Energy, Climate Change and Extractive Industries Program Director
Inter-American Dialogue

House Committee on Foreign Affairs
Subcommittee on Western Hemisphere
Hearing on Energy Opportunities in South America
May 17, 2017

I would like to thank the Committee and Subcommittee Chairmen and Ranking Members and the other committee members for the opportunity to be here today.

My testimony today will focus on the energy landscape in South America, the importance of US investment in oil and gas and clean energy in the region, and opportunities for energy policy engagement between the United States and South American countries.

The investment landscape for South American energy sectors

South America is an important destination for energy investment due to abundant natural resources, growing markets and favorable policy frameworks in many countries. The continent holds massive oil and gas reserves, from the Orinoco heavy oil belt in Venezuela to the deepwater presalt zone in Brazil and the Vaca Muerta shale play in Argentina. South America holds 20% of global proven crude oil reserves, or 330.1 billion barrels, and Venezuela has the largest proven oil reserves in the world. There is also abundant potential for renewable energy. The region has an estimated 430GW of unexploited hydropower potential. Brazil is the third largest country in the world for hydropower potential, only one third of which has been developed.

Additionally, South America has large domestic markets with rapidly growing consumption of oil for transportation and soaring demand for electricity. With strong economic growth and growing middle classes, Latin America overall is expected to see primary energy demand increase by 110 percent between 2000 and 2040, including a 183 percent rise in electricity demand and a 52 percent rise in oil demand.

Many countries have recently become more open to energy investments, enacting market-friendly policies and regulatory reforms to attract private capital and international expertise. New opportunities have opened up for private investment as more market-oriented leaders have come to power in Brazil and Argentina since late 2015. Since the collapse of global oil prices in mid-2014 many South American governments have offered increasingly favorable terms to draw investment after international oil companies cut exploration budgets.

Several South American countries also offer strong incentives for investment in renewables, such as wind and solar auctions, renewable portfolio standards, and favorable financing. South American countries have sought to expand non-hydroelectric renewable energy in response to numerous droughts and growing opposition to large hydroelectric dams because of social and environmental concerns. Wind and solar energy costs have fallen dramatically, reaching grid parity in multiple markets in the region. Legislation has also been approved in some countries to allow distributed generation.

In Brazil, President Michel Temer's government has opened opportunities for private investment in oil exploration and production by removing a requirement that Petrobras be the sole operator in all presalt fields and easing local content requirements. After virtually freezing oil licensing rounds for the last decade, Brazil is planning 10 oil and gas tenders over the next three years, including four in 2017. In the power sector, Brazil's development bank offers favorable financing for renewable energy projects, particularly solar.

In Argentina, investment in the oil and gas sector has accelerated since President Mauricio Macri took power in December 2015. Macri has taken steps to dismantle many of the long-standing barriers to private sector investment in Argentina, reducing subsidies for residential electricity consumers, eliminating currency controls and renegotiating labor costs with unions. Argentina also held its first two renewable energy auctions late last year under renewable energy program RenovAr.

Chile joined Brazil as one of the top ten renewable energy markets globally in 2015, almost doubling its share of renewables investment from 2014 and increasing installed capacity by 580 MW. In 2016, Chile attracted 84 participants to its renewable energy auction, resulting in the lowest price for solar PV projects globally at $29.10/MWh.

Colombia, seeking to maintain current levels of oil production and reserves despite the drop in prices, has offered very favorable investment terms. For example, the government has cut taxes on the oil sector, allowed companies to extend exploration and production periods, and reduced minimum investment requirements.

There are, however, exceptions to this generally more favorable investment climate in South America. Venezuela, marred by political upheaval and an economic crisis, has seen a sharp decline in investment in recent years. State oil company PDVSA has held majority stakes in oil projects since the industry was nationalized under former president Hugo Chavez, and the company controls operations and marketing for the bulk of its projects. PDVSA's joint venture partners have been frustrated by their inability to control operational decisions and to access their share of profits from oil sales. Private company partners have also seen their profits tumble because of exchange rate controls. Underinvestment has led to a steep decline in oil production -- output declined by 235,000 barrels per day in the first three quarters of last year and will likely drop below 2 million barrels per day before the end of the year. As a result, countries in Latin America and the Caribbean that have relied on imports of crude oil and refined products from Venezuela have turned to alternative oil suppliers and replaced oil with natural gas and renewable energy. Exports of Venezuelan oil to key partners such as Jamaica, the Dominican Republic, and even Cuba, have declined considerably.

In Ecuador, oil investors have largely pulled out since President Rafael Correa nationalized the industry in 2010 – with the notable exception of Andes Petroleum, a consortium of Chinese state oil companies. Ecuador's President-elect Lenin Moreno has yet to define his energy policy, and it is unclear whether he will reverse his predecessor's policies.

Even in countries such as Brazil, Colombia and Argentina, there are uncertainties over future energy policy. Brazil and Colombia will both elect new presidents next year, and Macri's energy policies have been unpopular and could come under threat.

The role of US investment in energy in South America

US investors and companies are key partners in developing energy resources and supplying markets in South America. US companies, which benefit from the human, technological, and financial resources of rapidly growing oil and renewable energy industries, as well as proximity to other countries in the hemisphere, have been at the forefront of the investment wave. US companies play an important role in bringing capital and expertise to produce oil and gas, generate power and build related infrastructure in the region.

US investment in energy brings multiple benefits to both the United States and South America. For South American governments, oil exports to the US market provide a critical source of revenue, and the development of energy resources is an economic driver for prosperity in the region. Investment in renewable energy brings environmental benefits. South America has the cleanest electricity matrix in the world, although several large cities face severe local air pollution due to heavy traffic and weak fuel efficiency and fuel quality standards. For the United States, energy investment in South America also has the potential to generate investment revenue and employment within the country.

Foreign investment also facilitates energy trade integration between the United States and its neighbors in South America. Despite the shale boom, which led to a 75 percent increase in US oil production over the past ten years and a drop in imports, the United States still relies on South America for about 20 percent of crude oil imports. Foreign investors are critical to developing oil resources in South America and to building midstream and downstream infrastructure to enable the flow of oil across the hemisphere. South America has also emerged as a key market for global LNG demand. The United States is projected to become a net natural gas exporter in 2018. A large number of US LNG export projects have already been approved by the Department of Energy but their ability to access financing and reach a final investment decision will depend on securing access to markets. US investment in energy infrastructure, such as power plants and natural gas pipelines in South America, can help create markets and spur demand for US natural gas.

However, US companies are by no means the only players, and if the United States cuts energy ties with South American countries, other actors will likely gain influence. China is a leading investor in oil and gas in many countries and is making inroads into hydropower and other renewable energy development. The China Development Bank and China Export-Import Bank have made more than $135 billion in loan commitments in South America since 2005, almost three quarters of which are focused on energy. China is second only to the United States as Latin America's largest source of greenfield FDI, and between 2011 and 2015, almost 40 percent of Chinese mergers and acquisitions investment in Latin America was in the oil and gas sector. Russia is also increasing its stake in Venezuela's oil industry. Chinese and Russian engagement in South America is largely viewed as driven by geopolitical as well as commercial interests.

Energy policy engagement between the United States and South America

While most US investment in South America's energy sectors has been market-driven, policy has also played a role in promoting energy integration and cross-border investment. A host of US government initiatives has been established over the past decade to assist other countries to develop regulatory standards that are in line with those of the United States. These initiatives have helped improve investment climates, create commercial opportunities for US companies and facilitate clear and consistent investment rules.

Collaboration on energy issues in turn helps bolster broader economic, political and security relations with South American countries, many of which serve as key allies for the United States and cooperate on a range of issues from immigration to counter-narcotics. The United States is also deeply integrated economically with South America; it is the top export market for many countries in the region, and South America is also a destination for many US goods and services.

Therefore it is important that the US government engage with Latin America on energy policy issues as part of broader bilateral relations. Strong diplomatic and economic ties, including free trade agreements, provide the foundation for energy trade and investment between the United States and South America. Within the energy sector specifically I would highlight two important areas of engagement.

First, in the oil sector, the United States should engage in regulatory cooperation and support reforms that enable private investment, such as the energy reforms in Brazil and Argentina. The United States should continue to engage in technical cooperation on regulations for shale oil development in Argentina and offshore exploration in Brazil and Colombia. Brazil and Colombia may also look to US assistance on best practices to develop their shale resources in the future. A critical aspect of this technical cooperation is on environmental regulations. The lack of a robust and efficient environmental regulatory process is a major obstacle to developing oil and gas resources in South America, and US experts in the Departments of Energy and the Interior as well as state regulators can share best practices on addressing this challenge.

Second, in clean energy, the United States could explore the creation of a working group on clean transportation with countries like Colombia, Brazil, Argentina and Chile. Reliable and sustainable transportation is one of the greatest challenges for many South American countries given the large degree of urbanization, rapidly growing transportation needs and critical problems with air pollution. The working group could share best practices in promoting higher fuel quality, fuel efficiency, urban mass transportation and electric mobility, which would be particularly beneficial in South America because of clean electricity generation.

In conclusion, given the importance of US energy relations with South America and indeed the rest of the hemisphere, it is critical to maintain energy policy engagement with US allies in the region. I look forward to the opportunity to respond to any questions or comments you may have.

Mr. DUNCAN. Thank you so much. Mr. Bordoff, you are recognized for 5 minutes.

STATEMENT OF MR. JASON BORDOFF, PROFESSOR AND DIRECTOR, CENTER ON GLOBAL ENERGY POLICY, SCHOOL OF INTERNATIONAL AND PUBLIC AFFAIRS, COLUMBIA UNIVERSITY

Mr. BORDOFF. Thank you, Chairman Duncan, Ranking Member Sires, and members of the committee. Thanks for the invitation to be here today.

It is certainly hard to survey all of South America in 5 minutes and so you have somewhat lengthy written testimony given the importance of this issue. I hope that will be helpful to the committee. But let me just summarize a few points in the 5 minutes that I have.

As you have already said, Mr. Chairman, and the other witnesses have said, South America plays a key role in global energy supply, trade, geopolitics. It is a net exporter of hydrocarbons. Venezuela has what may be the largest crude oil reserves in the world. Brazil alone could add well over 1 million barrels a day of oil supply over the next 5 years which may be crucial to keep a lid on oil prices, notwithstanding the low price environment that we are in today. And Argentina, as you have said, may be best positioned to replicate the shale revolution that we have seen in the U.S. South America also plays a leading role in clean energy technologies. The region produces more than 60 percent of its electricity from hydropower, along with rapidly growing solar and wind in different parts of the region.

Although the impacts of climate change, it should be noted, including more frequent droughts are actually threatening that clean energy resource of hydropower. So South America is acting to scale up its clean energy sources in lots of different ways.

South America is especially important I think for the U.S. because it is such a key energy trade partner with the U.S. and that is only growing. Two of the five largest sources of crude oil imports to the U.S. come from South America. It is also a growing market for U.S. energy exports as we have heard. Over the last decade, the U.S. has gone from the largest importer of refined petroleum products in the world to the largest exporter of refined petroleum products in the world. And about a quarter of that goes to South America. Because South American countries have failed to invest in refining, in effect, despite their very large oil reserves in effect, South America is sending its oil to the U.S. for us to turn into the useful products people want like gasoline, diesel, and then we send that back to South America.

We are also sending some oil to South America after the U.S. lifted its crude oil export ban, often used for blending as diluent with the heavier crudes that they have. And then Latin America has emerged as a key market. This was unexpected, a key market for U.S. LNG exports with a quarter of U.S. cargo so far making their way to Latin America, South America, about half if you include Mexico.

As for the oil and gas outlook, there are many opportunities, as well as challenges in the region. Jorge talked about the onerous regulatory and other terms. The pain of the oil price collapse I think has helped catalyze serious reform efforts to liberalize South America's energy sector, so countries are now taking steps to make themselves more competitive, more attractive to foreign investment which can help increase regional political stability, economic growth, global energy market stability. I talk about those in some detail in my written testimony.

Brazil, with some of the largest offshore resources in the world implementing reforms to reverse the damage done by years of resource nationalism and political turmoil and the corruption scandal at Petrobras. Argentina, pursuing reforms to attract technology and foreign investment for their shale. Venezuela, on the brink of complete collapse with really frightening potential implications for the health and safety of the people there, as well as regional political stability, not to mention the global oil market. Jorge mentioned that, too. The only point I would add I think that is an important reminder of why given the potential for disruptions like Venezuelan supply, it still remains a critical national security asset that we have a well-supplied strategic petroleum reserve, which I know there have been some efforts to reduce the size of recently in Congress.

And Colombia is working to attract investment and address environmental and indigenous concerns as they think about shale development. And that is not just oil and gas, obviously, but renewables. We see a lot of potential for further hydropower although it faces some opposition. Countries like Chile, Brazil, and Argentina have adopted regulatory reforms to boost renewables like solar and wind and these efforts, along with efforts to curb deforestation and land use related. Land use change related emissions I think are key to reducing greenhouse gas emissions and addressing the urgent threat of climate change.

So lastly, I would just note, I think, how important it is for the U.S. to continue to engage deeply and collaborate with South American countries as they pursue many of these efforts on economic diversification, to reduce their vulnerability to the inevitable boom/bust cycles that we have always seen, and will always see in oil markets. We need regulatory reform to attract much needed technology and foreign investment; safe and responsible energy development regulations to make sure production happens safely, not only to protect the environment, but also to build public trust and confidence and social license to operate so industry can go to work; more robust climate action, given how important it is to move more quickly with that; and then reduced energy demand and subsidy reform to reduce both fiscal strain on governments as well as reduce energy consumption and carbon emissions.

And with the right policies, I think the U.S. and South America have worked well together and can work even better together moving forward to develop the regions' energy potential and help meet our share of economic security and environmental goals.

So members of the committee, thanks again for inviting me today and I look forward to your questions.

environment.

[The prepared statement of Mr. Bordoff follows:]

COLUMBIA | SIPA
Center on Global Energy Policy

May 17, 2017

Congressional Testimony of

Jason E. Bordoff

Founding Director, Center on Global Energy Policy, and Professor of Professional Practice in International and Public Affairs, Columbia University School of International and Public Affairs

Before the

Committee on Foreign Affairs, Subcommittee on Western Hemisphere

United States House of Representatives

1st Session, 115th Congress

Chairman Duncan, Ranking Member Sires, and Members of the Committee, thank you for inviting me here today to discuss the energy outlook in South America. My name is Jason Bordoff. I am Professor of Professional Practice at Columbia University's School of International and Public Affairs and Founding Director of Columbia University SIPA's Center on Global Energy Policy. In my testimony, I will (1) summarize the importance of South America to the global energy system; (2) discuss the region's importance as an energy trading partner of the US; (3) provide an overview of opportunities for oil and gas and (4) of renewable energy in the region; and (5) offer a few thoughts on key areas of focus and potential partnership with the US if South America is to realize its energy opportunities.

Broadly speaking, the recent oil price collapse and economic strain throughout the region has helped to catalyze reform efforts to liberalize South America's energy sector. Countries in the region are now taking steps to make themselves more competitive and attractive to foreign investment. It is in the national interest of the US to help these countries succeed and develop their energy sectors in order to increase regional political stability and economic growth, promote global energy market stability, and open up new opportunities for investment of foreign capital from the US and elsewhere in the region. Many South American nations are also taking welcome steps to grow the share of low-carbon energy sources in their energy mix. Continued partnership to support cooperation on climate change is important to accelerate efforts to transition to a cleaner energy future.

South America's Importance to the Global Energy Landscape

South America plays an important role in global energy supply, trade and geopolitics. The region, as a whole, is a net exporter of fossil energy with a positive balance in oil, gas and coal alike. Venezuela is home to the world's largest crude oil reserves, larger even than those of Saudi Arabia.[1] Brazil alone could add well over a million barrels per day of oil production in the next five years, and deepwater production in Brazil—alongside US shale—may be key to meeting global oil demand growth and keeping a lid on oil prices in the foreseeable future. Argentina has the second largest technically

[1] As of end-2015, according to the BP Statistical Review of World Energy 2016.

Center on Global Energy Policy

recoverable shale gas and fourth largest tight oil resources in the world,[2] and the country is perhaps the best positioned to replicate something resembling the US shale revolution outside North America.

South America is also playing a leading role in clean energy technologies. In 2014, the region produced more than 60 percent of its electricity from renewable sources, compared with a world average of 22 percent, according to the International Energy Agency.[3] Most of this is hydropower, but there are reasons to be optimistic that other renewables can scale up in the coming years, including the region's prodigious solar and wind resource potential.

South America Is a Key Energy Trade Partner for the United States

South America is a key market for energy trade with the United States. As seen in Figure 1, the United States is a major recipient of South America's energy resources, although volumes have declined as US shale oil production has risen. Venezuela and Colombia are two of the five largest sources of America's crude oil imports, and South America, as a whole, accounted for 1.6 million b/d (or about a fifth) of our gross crude oil imports in 2016. (That rises to nearly 30 percent if Mexico is included.) The US Gulf Coast refineries are optimized for processing heavy or high sulfur crudes that make up a high percentage of exports from Venezuela and Mexico (and to a lesser degree Brazil and Colombia). Canada is a big competitor, and if the Keystone XL pipeline is completed, imports of heavy crudes from Latin America are likely to decline. We import relatively little coal as a share of our total consumption (~1.4 percent),[4] but 80 percent of these imports come from South America, most of it from Colombia.[5]

[2] U.S. Energy Information Administration, "World Shale Resource Assessment," *EIA*, September 24, 2015, https://www.eia.gov/analysis/studies/worldshalegas/.

[3] International Energy Agency, "IEA World Energy Outlook 2016," *IEA*, p.552 and p.620.

[4] EIA, "(2016) Table ES-1 U.S. Coal Summary Statistics, 2010-2016," *EIA Quarterly Coal Report, October-December 2016*, https://www.eia.gov/coal/production/quarterly/pdf/tes1p01p1.pdf.

[5] EIA, "(2016) Table 18 U.S. Coal Imports," *EIA Quarterly Coal Report, October-December 2016*, https://www.eia.gov/coal/production/quarterly/pdf/t18p01p1.pdf.

COLUMBIA | SIPA
Center on Global Energy Policy

Figure 1. US Crude Oil Imports from Latin America (million barrels per day)

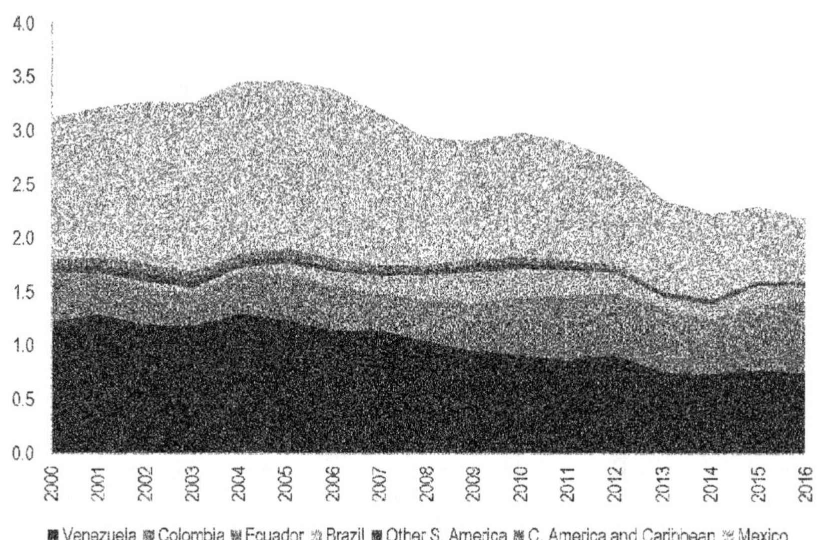

Source: EIA

As seen in Figure 2, Latin America is also an important and growing market for US energy exports, particularly refined products and—increasingly—liquefied natural gas (LNG). Over the last decade, the US has gone from being the largest importer of refined petroleum in the world to the largest exporter of refined petroleum. A little less than a third (or about 1.4 million b/d) of our refined petroleum product exports go to South America and the Caribbean, and just about half (or about 2.3 million b/d out of 4.7 million b/d) if one includes Mexico.[6] Despite their large crude oil reserves, many South American countries have failed to invest in refining due to the lack of capital to build expensive infrastructure, cost overruns, and market uncertainty. The fact that many countries in the region have subsidized domestic fuel prices has made refining investment unattractive, especially for national oil companies with upstream priorities that are short of cash. Moreover, technical problems and poor maintenance mean that many existing refineries operate far below capacity.[7] There is also a growing mismatch between the heavier oil many countries produce and what their refineries can process, forcing them to import light oil and other diluents. Some of Latin America's largest NOCs, on the other hand, have made substantial investments in US refineries. Venezuela's PDVSA owns

[6] EIA, "Exports by Destination," *EIA Petroleum and other Liquids,* Apr 28, 2017, https://www.eia.gov/dnav/pet/pet_move_expc_a_EPP0_EEX_mbblpd_a.htm.

[7] Lisa Viscidi, "Filling the Gap: How the US Energy Boom is Shaping Latin American Refining Markets," Inter-American Dialogue, March 2015, p.5-6, http://www.thedialogue.org/wp-content/uploads/2015/06/Filling-the-Gap-web-Lisa-Viscidi-March-2015.pdf.

Citgo in the US with 749,000 b/d of refining capacity,[8] and Pemex owns half of the Deer Park refinery (in a joint venture (JV) with Shell) with 340,000 b/d of capacity.[9]

Figure 2. US Refined Product Exports to Latin America (million barrels per day)

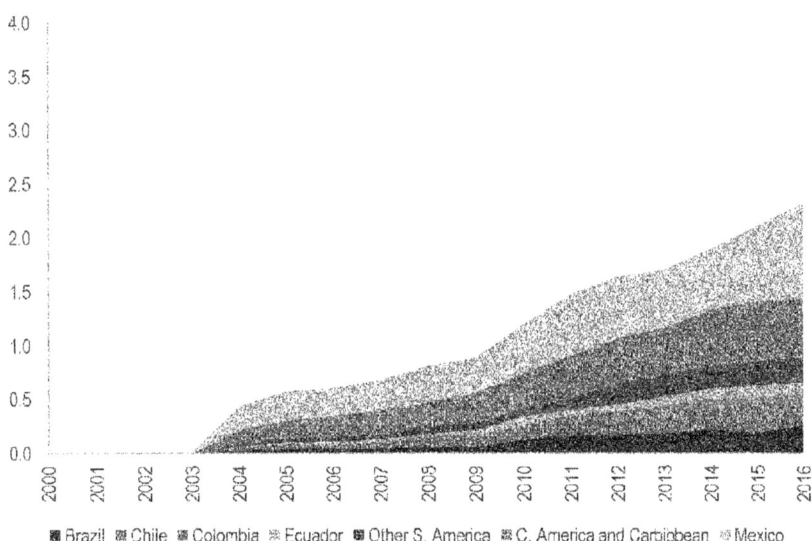

Source: EIA

In effect, our complex refineries in the Gulf Coast and California take crude oil from Latin America, refine it into valuable petroleum products (such as gasoline and diesel) at a fairly high profit, and sell it back to consumers across South America, where refining capacity falls far short of local demand. US Gulf Coast refineries are much better-positioned to supply the South American market with products than competitors overseas because US refiners benefit from lower fuel costs (thanks to cheap shale gas) and because of their physical proximity to the region. Exports to Latin America, in turn, play a key role in the profitability of US Gulf Coast refiners.[10]

After the US lifted its oil export ban, Latin America became a destination for US light crude exports. In 2016, about 12 percent of total US crude exports went to this region. Given that much of South American production in countries like Venezuela and Colombia is of heavy crude, this light oil from the US may well find its way back to America after being blended with heavy oil to make South

[8] Gordon Meghan, "US Congress calls for CFIUS review of Rosneft's potential stake in Citgo," *S&P Global Platts*, Apr 7, 2017, https://www.platts.com/latest-news/oil/washington/us-congress-calls-for-cfius-review-of-rosnefts-21395865.
[9] "About Deer Park," *About Us Shell in U.S.*, Shell, 3 Oct. 2016, http://www.shell.us/about-us/projects-and-locations/deer-park-manufacturing-site/about-shell-deer-park.html.
[10] Housley Carr, "Livin' La Vida Local - U.S. Distillate Exports From Gulf Coast To Latin America On The Rise," RBN Energy, May 10, 2017, https://rbnenergy.com/livin-la-vida-local-us-distillate-exports-to-latin-america-on-the-rise.

American grades suitable for processing in Gulf Coast refineries.

As Figure 3 shows, Latin America has also emerged as a market of choice for US LNG cargoes since the first LNG export terminal at Sabine Pass started operations in February 2016. Through April 2017, about a quarter of the 100-odd cargoes that were lifted from Sabine Pass went to South America, or nearly half if we include Mexico. This is quite a departure from the expectation a few years ago that most US LNG exports would find their way to the Asian market, given the high price of Asian LNG at the time. The ability for US LNG to shift from one destination to another, based on commercial considerations, is a key feature of US LNG exports that is making the global natural gas market more competitive, secure, and efficient.[11]

Figure 3: Destinations of US LNG Export Cargoes to Date (February 2016 through April 2017)

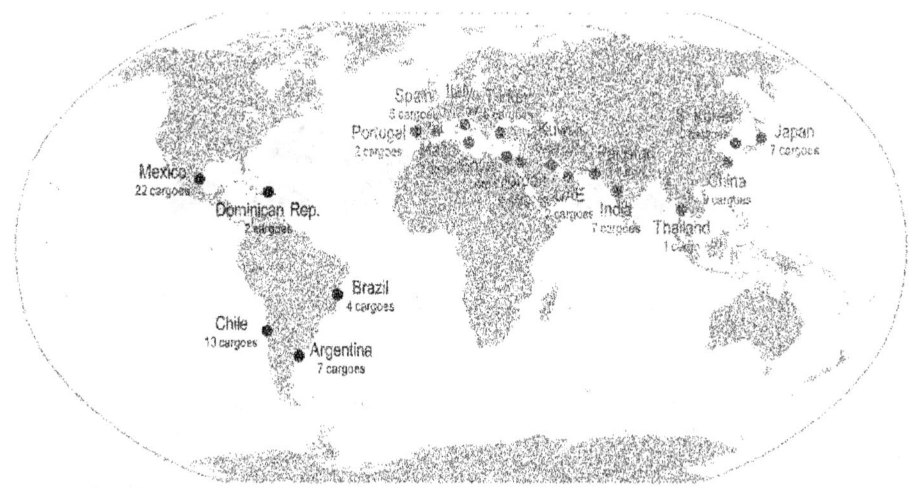

Source: Bloomberg

The region's potential as a destination for US LNG cargoes is set to increase over time. As production ramps up at US LNG export terminals, America will soon eclipse Qatar as the biggest source of flexible LNG supply that can go anywhere in the world, depending on the price.[12] As I have argued previously, US LNG will make the global gas market more flexible, more liquid and more integrated, thanks to the unique structure of US LNG contracts.[13] Floating storage and

---

[11] Jason Bordoff and Akos Losz (2016), "The Benign Energy Superpower? The United States Turns On the Gas," *Foreign Affairs*, March 4, 2016, https://www.foreignaffairs.com/ articles/2016-03-04/united-states-turns-gas.

[12] Jason Bordoff and Akos Losz (2016), "If you build it, will they come? The competitiveness of US LNG in overseas markets," Center on Global Energy Policy, Columbia SIPA, November 2016, p.7-8, http://energypolicy.columbia.edu/sites/default/files/energy/Competitiveness%20of%20US%20LNG%20in%20Overseas%20Markets.pdf.

[13] Jason Bordoff and Akos Losz (2016), "The Benign Energy Superpower? The United States Turns On the Gas," *Foreign Affairs*, March 4, 2016, https://www.foreignaffairs.com/ articles/2016-03-04/united-states-turns-gas

regasification (FSRU) technology has recently emerged as the quickest, cheapest and most flexible way to take advantage of this newfound supply, enabling emerging economies to import gas at a fraction of the time and cost than would be the case with traditional onshore LNG import terminals. South America is already the biggest regional market in terms of floating LNG regasification capacity, and this will further expand with the addition of at least two new FSRU terminals (in Brazil and Uruguay) over the next few years.[14] Colombia has recently joined the ranks of LNG importing countries, with the addition of a new floating terminal earlier this year.[15]

Oil and Gas Opportunities in South America

South America has the potential to be an important source of future energy supply, yet oil production has been stagnant or falling in many countries in the region (Figure 4). Falling output, combined with the recent oil price collapse, has severely strained many South American countries, providing a catalyst to undertake much-needed reforms to attract foreign investment. As Figure 5 shows, perceptions of policy risk remain a barrier to investment in much of South America.

Figure 4. Oil Production in Selected Latin American Countries (million barrels per day)

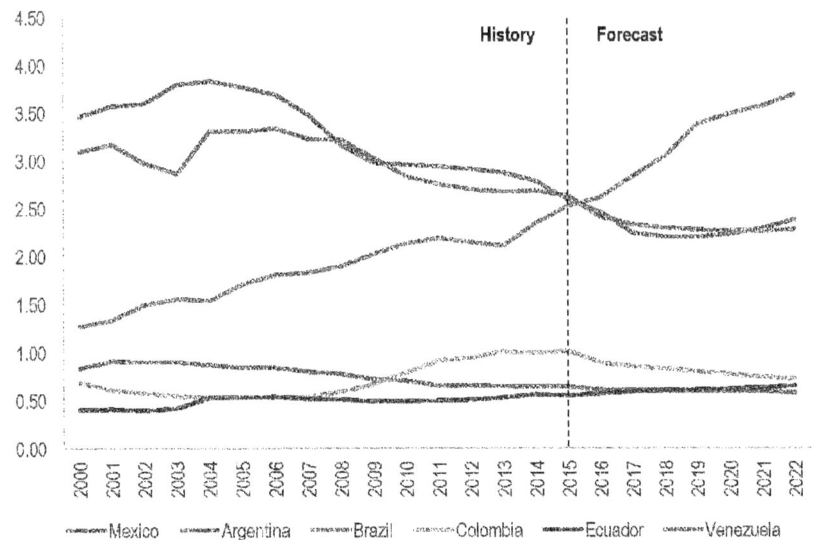

Source: BP Statistical Review of World Energy, IEA

[14] Wood MacKenzie, "Global LNG - FSRU overview 2017," April 2017, p.5 and p.9
[15] International Gas Union, "2017 World LNG Report", *International Gas Union*, April 5, 2017, p.5, http://www.igu.org/news/igu-releases-2017-world-lng-report

Figure 5: Fraser Institute Global Petroleum Survey 2015 – Policy Perception index

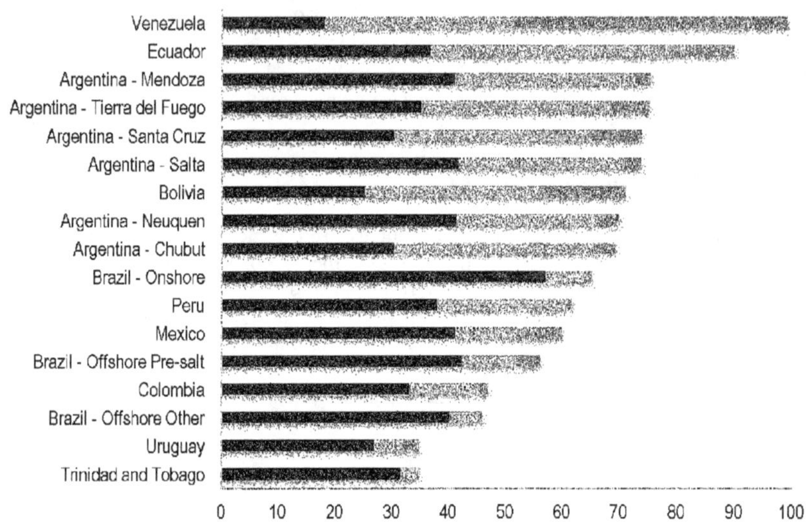

Source: Fraser Institute

Brazil

For oil supply, Brazil's deepwater "pre-salt" oil resources are among the most attractive oil assets in the world, and economical to develop even at today's relatively low oil price levels.[16] The International Energy Agency projects Brazilian production to grow by more than 1 million b/d by 2022. But with recent regulatory changes, others are even more bullish.[17]

While impressive, even this outlook is a far cry from what many had forecasted a few years ago.[18] In a special section of the World Energy Outlook (WEO) in 2013, the IEA projected Brazil's oil output would reach 4.1 million b/d in 2020 and 6 million b/d in 2035.[19] The most recent WEO now projects production of 3.1 and 4.4 million b/d in those years, respectively.[20] Moreover, Brazil's

[16] Sabrina Valle and Peter Millard, "Petrobras Says Deep-Water Opening Luring Big Oil to Brazil," *Bloomberg Markets*, Oct 10, 2016, https://www.bloomberg.com/news/articles/2016-10-10/petrobras-says-deep-water-opening-luring-big-oil-to-brazil.
[17] Citi Research, for example, is projecting a roughly 2 million b/d rise through 2022. See Citi Commodities Research, "Energy 2022: Return of the Unconventionals," February 1, 2017, p.49.
[18] Petrobras's 2011 Business Plan projected Brazilian oil production to reach 4.9 million barrels per day by 2020. See http://www.investidorpetrobras.com.br/download/1575, p.18.
[19] IEA, "IEA World Energy Outlook 2013," *IEA*, p.481.
[20] IEA, "IEA World Energy Outlook 2016," *IEA*, p.136.

legacy fields have some of the steepest decline rates in the world, further hampering efforts to grow the nation's output.

Brazil's energy sector has been hampered for several years by the moves toward resource nationalism undertaken by the Rouseff administration, forcing Petrobras to be the operator and have 30 percent equity in all pre-salt projects, subsidizing the domestic market, imposing stringent local content requirements (often subject to corruption), and swapping reserves for equity in Petrobras. The market capitalization of the firm dropped from a peak of more than $300 billion in 2008 to less than $20 billion in early-2016, before recovering to around $67 billion today.[21]

More recently, Brazil's energy sector has suffered from the controversy preceding the impeachment of former President Dilma Rousseff last year and the epic corruption scandal at Petrobras. Petrobras is financially crippled by the largest debt burden in the global oil industry, and plans to sell off assets and reduce costs to bring that debt burden down. It has made some progress in doing so, as evidenced by the company's latest quarterly earnings report. Petrobras is ahead of schedule to meet its target of reducing net debt to 2.5 times earnings before interest, tax and depreciation (EBITDA), from 3.2 at the end of March 2017 and 5.1 in 2015.[22] Asset sales amounted to $13.6 billion in 2016, somewhat short of the company's $15 billion target,[23] and Petrobras is planning divestments totaling $21 billion in 2017 and 2018.[24]

In the aftermath of the corruption scandal engulfing Petrobras and much of the country's oil and gas sector, Petrobras's new CEO, Pedro Parente, has developed a strategic plan to restructure the company and reform its policies to deliver more accountability and transparency. The Brazilian government has introduced wide-ranging regulatory reforms to attract more foreign investment in the country's energy sector, which it views as key to boosting oil output and supporting an economic recovery. The reforms were aimed at changing the government's previously tight control over deepwater developments. International oil companies can now be the operators of deepwater projects—a role that was previously reserved for Petrobras in the most prolific areas. Local content requirements, which previously held back field development, have been eased, and the government plans as many as 10 bid rounds for new exploration blocks over the next three years.[25] While the reforms have been promising, obstacles remain, including ambiguity about local content rules and different treatment of new versus current licenses.

Reform efforts hold promise to not only help boost Brazil's output, but also open up new opportunities in Brazil's deepwater province for foreign oil companies, investment funds and service companies. For example, Statoil paid $2.5 billion for a 66 percent stake in the Caracara pre-salt field, and Total paid S2.2 billion for a package of assets that included a 22.5 percent stake in the Iara fields

---

21 "Petrobras Market Cap," *Y Charts*, May 16, 2017, https://ycharts.com/companies/PBR/market_cap.

22 Marta Nogueira and Rodrigo Viga Gaier, "Record Petrobras Operating Profit Speeds Debt Reduction," *Reuters*, May 11, 2017, http://www.reuters.com/article/us-petrobras-results-idUSKBN187352.

23 Luciano da Costa,and Tatiana Bautzer, "Brazil's Petrobras says Missed 2015-2016 Asset Sale Target," *Reuters Africa*, Dec 28, 2016, http://af.reuters.com/article/commoditiesNews/idAFE6N14A03Y.

24 Investor Relations Press Release, "New Divestment Portfolio," *Investor Relations PetroBras*, May 10, 2017, http://www.investidorpetrobras.com.br/en/press-releases/new-divestment-portfolio.

25 Stephen Rassenfoss, "OTC: Brazil Energy Reforms Yield Big Lease Sales and Questions," *Journal of Petroleum Technology*, May 2, 2017, https://www.spe.org/en/jpt/jpt-article-detail/?art=2946.

and an operating 35 percent stake in the Lapa projects.[26] The reforms present new opportunities for US firms to invest as well, perhaps through joint ventures with other foreign oil companies active in Brazil.

The oil price collapse has undermined Brazil's outlook as well, although Petrobras estimates its pre-salt breakevens at around $45 per barrel (and others put it even lower). These are among the most attractive deepwater prospects in the world, although the breakeven prices and risks in Brazil remain high compared with the rest of the region, including shale. Mexico's deepwater prospects could also be a formidable competitor. Nonetheless, Brazil stands out in the region (along with Mexico) for the credibility of its new institutional framework and for attracting so much new foreign investment.

Looking forward, the International Energy Agency and others have warned that sharp cutbacks in capital investments in the oil sector during the price collapse of the last two years means that new supply may not be developed to meet rising demand. Notwithstanding the likely rapid rise of shale, oil markets could be tight by the end of the decade. If demand growth remains even moderately strong, US shale oil alone likely will not be sufficient to meet it, and higher prices could trigger even more investment in unconventional resources like Brazil's pre-salt fields.

While Brazil had been self-sufficient in natural gas through the end of the 1990s, it has since imported growing volumes of Bolivian pipeline gas and, more recently, LNG. Development of the pre-salt oil reserves will also yield large volumes of associated gas, and developing the necessary infrastructure to accommodate that gas remains a challenge. A major expansion of deepwater production will require some combination of offshore evacuation infrastructure, onshore gas processing, greater domestic demand, and LNG export facilities. Whether domestic politics may limit export opportunities in the face of rising domestic import needs, as seen in other countries, is another political risk for international firms.

Argentina

The success of Argentina's shale oil and gas developments also crucially depends on foreign capital and technology. The country's Vaca Muerta shale play is one of the most promising shale resources in the world.[27] The area has seen increased activity in recent years, not least thanks to the active participation of international oil majors, such as Chevron, ExxonMobil and Shell, as well as the major US-based oilfield service companies, such as Halliburton, Baker Hughes and Schlumberger. After several years of shale drilling, the performance of the most recently drilled wells rivals that of the Eagle Ford shale formation in the US, according to Morgan Stanley, and horizontal drilling is economically viable at today's prices and drilling costs.[28] Horizontal well costs have fallen by half since 2015—although significant infrastructure, management, and cost issues remain.[29]

---

[26] Justin Jacobs, "Trying to right the Petrobras ship," *Petroleum Economist*, March 8, 2017.
[27] Philippe A. Charlez, "Geopolitics of Unconventional Resources Outside North America," Society of Petroleum Engineers, 2016, p.3-5, https://www.onepetro.org/conference-paper/SPE-181405-MS.
[28] Morgan Stanley Research, "YPF's Vaca Muerta: Alive and Kicking!," *Morgan Stanley*, March 29, 2017, p.4.
[29] Goldman Sachs Equity Research, "YPF Sociedad Anónima (YPF): Assessing productivity/efficiencies in Vaca Muerta; 1Q2017 preview," *Goldman Sachs*, May 9, 2017.

COLUMBIA | SIPA
Center on Global Energy Policy

Four years after the first pilot project, shale production reached 62,000 barrels of oil equivalent per day, representing around 5 percent of Argentina's output.[30] This growth was achieved in the face of a challenging political, regulatory and oil market environment, which is improving. Moreover, just as US shale output was consistently underestimated, it is reasonable to expect that technology and productivity improvements will bring down costs and increase the production potential in Argentina as well. Fewer than 100 horizontal wells have been drilled in the Vaca Muerta, compared with nearly 20,000 in the Eagle Ford.

Nevertheless, ramping up production at Vaca Muerta will require a sharp increase in drilling and foreign investment. Developing Vaca Muerta's shale resources requires capital expenditures of between $10-15 billion annually, according to industry estimates. Foreign investment also brings much-needed technology and expertise. (Shell's CEO Ben van Beurden recently spoke at the CERAWeek industry conference in Houston about the company's first remotely-drilled well in Argentina's Vaca Muerta play, which was controlled by Shell engineers sitting in Calgary. This well was also Shell's cheapest horizontal well in Argentina at the time).[31]

Attracting foreign investment will require continued improvement in the political and regulatory landscape—especially given the competition for capital investments from other regions with attractive oil and gas resources. Political risk has long loomed as a major risk in Argentina, as seen with the prior administration's renationalization of YPF from Repsol in 2012. The country has one of the worst historical records for respecting oil contracts in the industry and is notorious for its political volatility. One advantage of shale is that sunk costs are smaller and capital recovery is faster than in conventional oil production, so the expropriation risks are comparably lower.

Argentina's legislative elections in October 2017 represent a key milestone for the continuity of the Macri administration's reform program. Rigid labor contracts have been seen as a driver of low productivity, but unions recently agreed to make changes in new contracts for unconventional oil and gas activities aimed at boosting productivity and lowering drilling costs. More broadly, Argentina's political and economic challenges over the last several years, including the lack of access to financial markets, have adversely impacted the business and investment climate. The current government is undertaking much-needed macro and fiscal adjustments, but economic challenges at home remain an obstacle. The government has also maintained artificially high crude oil and pump prices with the goal of stimulating production and employment, but history, including in the US, shows that price controls do more harm than good over time, and markets will need to be liberalized.[32]

Unconventional gas in Argentina is still in early stages, but the government is trying to promote foreign investment with a pricing incentive scheme. Boosting Argentina's gas output is key to reduce

[30] Morgan Stanley Research, "YPF's Vaca Muerta: Alive and Kicking!," *Morgan Stanley*, March 29, 2017, p.4.
[31] "Oil Struggles to Enter the Digital Age," *The Economist*, April 6, 2017, http://www.economist.com/news/business/21720338-talk-digital-oil-rig-may-be-bit-premature-oil-struggles-enter-digital-age.
[32] Jason Bordoff (2016), "America's Energy Policy - From Independence to Interdependence," *Horizons: Journal of International Relations and Sustainable Development*, Autumn 2016, Issue No. 9, http://www.cirsd.org/en/horizons/horizons-autumn-2016--issue-no-8/americas-energy-policy-from-independence-to-interdependence.

a growing dependence on imported gas—quite a turnaround from its position as a net gas exporter prior to 2004. As one example, the Argentina-Chile gas pipeline was built 20 years ago to supply Chile's gas needs from Argentinian production, but is now used to transport gas imported by Chile as LNG, to Argentina. Given a decade-long decline in domestic gas production, Argentina relies on costly LNG and imported gas from Bolivia for more than one-fifth of its gas use. This is not only a drag on the economy, but also presents energy security concerns. Boosting shale oil and gas output has the potential to eliminate Argentina's sizeable energy trade deficit, which has gone from a $6 billion surplus to a $6 billion deficit over the last decade.[33] The government incentive program that pays $7.50 per million BTU for gas production has been extended through 2018 at the current rate, and will be gradually reduced to $6 per million BTU by 2021 before market prices take effect from 2022.[34]

Another key to reducing this energy trade deficit is curbing domestic demand in Argentina. The Macri administration is aiming to do that through increases of gas and electricity tariffs towards international levels. Liberalization of gas and power prices has been at the heart of the country's macroeconomic adjustment.[35] Eliminating fossil fuel energy consumption subsidies is a welcome development, as it not only eases strain on government coffers (gas subsidies cost the government $5.7 billion in 2015),[36] but also reduces energy use and greenhouse gas emissions.[37] Although the Macri administration has slowed the pace of price adjustments, it is still aiming for full liberalization by the end of the administration's first term in office.

Venezuela

As this committee knows well, Venezuela is on the brink. The situation in Venezuela is tragic, as the nation descends further into crisis, and it could completely unravel into even more violence and chaos at any moment. The consequences matter enormously for the health and safety of the Venezuelan people, for the stability and economies of neighboring countries, and for global oil markets and US dependence on Venezuelan heavy oil.

Venezuela has the largest oil reserves in the world,[38] but the oil price collapse, falling production, and chronic mismanagement of PDVSA and the wider economy has contributed to severe economic crisis, rapid inflation, and shortages of food, medicine and other basic goods. The

[33] Morgan Stanley Research, "YPF's Vaca Muerta: Alive and Kicking!," *Morgan Stanley*, March 29, 2017, p.21.

[34] Charles Newbery, "Argentina's Tecpetrol Plan 150-well Vaca Muerta Gas Program," *S&P Global Platts*, March 23, 2017, https://www.platts.com/latest-news/natural-gas/buenosaires/argentinas-tecpetrol-plans-150-well-vaca-muerta-21249905.

[35] Benedict Mander, "Argentina Raises Electricity Tariffs by up to 148% to Fight Deficit," *Financial Times*, January 31, 2017, https://www.ft.com/content/fa0718c7-a223-3af5-a1c3-4c3f885697a3.

[36] "Argentina Proposes 203 pct. Hike in Natural Gas Prices at Public Hearing," *Hoy – The San Diego Union Tribune*, September 16, 2016, http://www.sandiegouniontribune.com/hoy-san-diego/sdhoy-argentina-proposes-203-pct-hike-in-natural-gas-2016sep16-story.html.

[37] Toshiyuki Shirai, "Commentary: Putting the Right Price on Energy", *International Energy Agency*, April 27, 2017, https://www.iea.org/newsroom/news/2017/april/commentary-putting-the-right-price-on-energy.html.

[38] Note that many experts believe Venezuela's oil reserves are vastly overstated and mostly consist of extra-heavy oil—although even if adjustments are made, Venezuela still has some of the largest reserves in the world.

Center on Global Energy Policy

accumulated decline in GDP is estimated at 26 percent since 2013.[39] In what was once Latin America's richest country, people are now starving and dying of easily treatable illnesses.[40] Venezuela depends on oil for more than 90 percent of export revenues.

Venezuela already poses a major risk to world oil markets, with production slipping from around 2.4 million b/d last year to around 2 million b/d today. A crippling electricity crisis last year threatened PDVSA operations, and severe cash constraints mean that PDVSA struggles to maintain its oil export terminals, refineries and other infrastructure. Although it has tried hard to attract foreign investment, the outlook is bleak.

The strain of low oil prices on PDVSA's finances threaten an even more crippling impact on the company's production moving forward.[41] PDVSA is already in arrears with suppliers and JV partners, preventing much needed investment to maintain supply. PDVSA may well default later this year. If it does, oil production could be expected to decline even more steeply, as it would struggle to import diluent to mix with Venezuelan heavy crude, or pay for essential oilfield service operations.

At the heart of PDVSA's financial strains are high bond debt service payments which the company has prioritized against payment to other creditors and suppliers. PDVSA fears that a default could lead to disruption of its tankers or receivables from disgruntled bondholders wanting to seize Venezuelan assets abroad. But inability to continue financing itself forced PDVSA into a debt swap last year, and the company had to put up its refinery assets in the US as collateral for the transaction. The Russian oil company Rosneft also received a minority share of Citgo, owned by Venezuela, as collateral for its $1.5 billion loan to PDVSA last year. A potential consequence of default may be that Rosneft takes control of Citgo, a major refiner in the US.[42] As this Committee has emphasized in the past, the potential energy security implications of such a development warrant immediate scrutiny by the Trump Administration.

Two months into street protests, there is much more talk of regime change. The government's severe financial strain makes it more difficult to buy the support of the military. The opposition appears more united than ever, and President Maduro's decisions, like calling a constitutional assembly, have fueled protests even further.

Although oil markets today are buffered by high inventory levels, further disruptions in Venezuela's oil output pose risks of potential oil price spikes in the years ahead, which would thus impact US

---

[39] IMF World Economic Outlook Database, *IMF*, April 2017, https://www.imf.org/external/pubs/ft/weo/2017/01/weodata/index.aspx.

[40] Juan Forero, "Venezuela is Starving", *The Wall Street Journal*, May 5, 2017, https://www.wsj.com/articles/venezuela-is-starving-1493995317.

[41] Luisa Palacios (2016), "Venezuela's Growing Risk to the Oil Market," Center on Global Energy Policy, August 2016, p.3, http://energypolicy.columbia.edu/sites/default/files/energy/CGEP_VENEZUELA'S%20GROWING%20RISK%20TO%20THE%20OIL%20MARKET_August%202016.pdf.

[42] Meghan Gordon, "US Congress Calls for CFIUS Review of Rosneft's Potential Stake in Citgo," *S&P Global Platts*, April 7, 2017, https://www.platts.com/latest-news/oil/washington/us-congress-calls-for-cfius-review-of-rosnefts-21395865.

consumers at the pump—yet another reason why the US Strategic Petroleum Reserve remains a vital national security asset despite the recent decline in US oil imports resulting from the shale boom.[43]

Colombia

Colombia has enjoyed a remarkable transformation in its oil and gas sector since regulatory reforms in 2003 turned around declining production. These included Ecopetrol's transition from a state-owned company to an independent and integrated entity, the creation of an independent regulatory agency, and the shift from production sharing contracts to a concession-based regime based on taxes and royalties. In response, oil production nearly doubled from 2005 to 2013.

But today, the oil and gas sector again faces declining output and reserves. Many nations have suffered from the fall in oil prices, but oil field capex in Colombia has fallen at an especially rapid rate. With projections for continued production declines, the government is actively seeking ways to attract more investment with new fiscal incentives offshore. The historic peace agreement with FARC also paves the way to a new era of security and prosperity that can attract further investment into Colombia's energy sector. At the same time, however, the incorporation into the political process of former rebel groups (namely FARC and ELN), which are opposed to foreign investment, may present a barrier to continued inflows of outside capital. As new governance arrangements take hold, it will be important to balance the need for consultation with local communities with the need for industry to have a clear understanding of the regulatory and licensing process moving forward so they can plan and invest.

Colombia also has substantial unconventional oil and gas resource potential with current exploration activities concentrated in the Middle Magdalena Basin. Yet the development of unconventional resources faces intense opposition from environmental, indigenous and other groups.[44] Colombia's Environment Minister recently said the country may not be ready for shale development, although he was reportedly rebuked by President Santos, sending conflicting signals about the government's position.[45] If Colombia is to develop its shale resources, the government will need to maintain a strong regulatory regime aimed at safe and responsible production and engage with local communities to address their important concerns. At the same time, to encourage private sector investment, it should also implement regulations consistently, provide a stable regulatory regime, and enforce existing laws.

In early May, Ecopetrol announced a major offshore gas discovery in Colombia's Caribbean Sea—the largest find in Colombia's oil and gas sector in three decades.[46] President Santos trumpeted the

---

[43] Jason Bordoff (2015), Congressional Testimony Before the Committee on Energy and Natural Resources, United States Senate, 1st Session, 114th Congress, October 6, 2015, https://www.energy.senate.gov/public/index.cfm/files/serve?File_id=6ffc0bd9-49b8-485d-b961-439ac6b38bd2.

[44] Alianza Colombiana Libre de Fracking, "To: President Juan Manuel Santos Calderon," March 27, 2017, https://redjusticiaambientalcolombia.files.wordpress.com/2017/03/2017-03-14-carta-presidente-santos_finalconlogos.pdf.

[45] "Colombia No Esta Preparada para el Fracking, Dice MinAmbiente," RCN *Radio*, March 22, 2017, http://www.rcnradio.com/medioambiente/colombia-no-esta-preparada-para-el-fracking-dice-minambiente/.

[46] Chris Kraul, "Colombian President Announces Largest Gas Find in Decades," *S&P Global Platts*, May 3, 2017, https://www.platts.com/latest-news/natural-gas/bogota/colombian-president-announces-largest-gas-find-21625450.

find in a televised press conference and said it would enable Colombia to be self-sufficient in gas in the coming years.[47] Colombia's gas production has declined in recent years, and it is projected to be a net importer in the near future.[48] New sources of gas supply, from shale or offshore, have the potential to meet Colombia's rising demand with domestic resources.

Other

It is beyond the scope of this testimony to go into detail into the outlook for every South American country. Other countries to note include Guyana[49] and Suriname,[50] with the offshore areas of these countries emerging as one of the region's top deepwater frontiers—although the dispute with Venezuela over claims to the offshore territory will need to be resolved. Chile also holds much promise as a new shale gas province.[51]

Renewable Energy Opportunities

South America is not only important for fossil fuel production and trade, but it is also an important growth region for renewable energy. The region already generates more than 60 percent of its power from renewable sources, the highest in the world, according to the IEA.[52] The vast majority of this comes from large hydropower plants. In 2015, Brazil generated 60 percent of its electricity from hydropower alone. The same share was as high as 74 percent in Uruguay and Costa Rica in 2015. However, further large-scale hydropower developments are increasingly constrained by reliability issues,[53] as was demonstrated during Brazil's multi-year drought between 2014 and 2016.[54]

In South America more than in any other region in the world, the reliability of large amounts of zero-carbon energy is being negatively affected by the unfolding impacts of climate change. Droughts have become increasingly frequent and severe, so water is not always available when needed. Moreover, hydropower is challenged by growing public opposition against hydro projects in

---

47 "Latest Find off Colombia Could Delineate New Gas Province," *Newsbase*, Ed. Ryan Stevenson, Week 18, Issue. 662, May 9, 2017, http://newsbase.com/topstories/latest-find-colombia-could-delineate-new-gas-province.

48 Anouk Honoré (2016), "South American Gas Markets and the role of LNG," Oxford Institute for Energy Studies, October 2016, p.127-129, https://www.oxfordenergy.org/wpcms/wp-content/uploads/2016/10/South-American-Gas-Markets-and-the-Role-of-LNG-NG-114.pdf.

49 Clifford Krauss, "With a Major Oil Discovery, Guyana is Poised to Become Top Producer," *The New York Times*, January 13, 2017, https://www.nytimes.com/2017/01/13/business/energy-environment/major-oil-find-guyana-exxon-mobile-hess.html.

50 Ed Crooks and Andres Schipani, "Guyana oil prospects stir friction between Venezuela and Exxon Mobile," *The Financial Times*, March 20, 2017, https://www.ft.com/content/013bfd26-0a8e-11e7-ac5a-903b21361b43.

51 "Conoco Phillips eyes Chile and Colombia," *UpStream*, http://www.upstreamonline.com/hardcopy/1192210/conocophillips-eyes-chile-and-colombia.

52 IEA, "Medium-Term Renewable Energy Market Report 2016", *IEA*, p.80.

53 Slade Johnson and Kirstin Berndt, "Hydroelectric Plants Account for more than 70% of Brazil's Electric Generation," Today in Energy – *EIA*, August 11, 2016, https://www.eia.gov/todayinenergy/detail.php?id=27472.

54 Caroline Stauffer, "Drought ends in Brazil's Sao Paulo but future still uncertain," *Reuters*, February 18, 2016, http://www.reuters.com/article/us-brazil-water-idUSKCN0VR1YJ.

environmentally sensitive areas. Brazil and Chile have recently had to cancel major dam projects on environmental grounds.[55]

Non-hydro renewables currently represent a small portion (less than 10 percent) of the region's electricity mix. But solar and wind capacity have seen healthy growth in recent years and are set to expand further at a rapid pace in the medium-term, not least thanks to the region's excellent wind and solar resources.[56] The IEA predicts that wind capacity will increase 2.4-fold between 2015 and 2021 across the region, while solar PV capacity is expected to grow more than 6-fold over the same period.[57] Renewable developers in the region face a host of challenges, including high interest rates, financing difficulties and macroeconomic risks (in the aftermath of recessions in Brazil and Argentina in 2016) as well as a lack of grid interconnectivity in many parts of the region. The lack of gas-fired generation capacity and pipeline infrastructure—which could be an important means to balance the intermittent energy supply from solar or wind—can also hinder the deployment of wind and solar power across the region.[58] If these issues can be resolved then the IEA reckons that the region, as a whole, could see 20 percent more renewable capacity additions through 2021 than in the agency's base case.

Countries such as Chile, Brazil, Mexico and Argentina have recently adopted regulatory reforms to encourage renewable energy without subsidies. Chile, for example, has encouraged renewable investment by auctioning smaller contracts, and has a regulatory framework trusted by investors. It has set a target of producing 20 percent of its electricity from non-hydro renewable sources by 2025. In Argentina, the Macri administration has also placed its bets on renewable energy. Congress last year passed a bill aimed at increasing the share of renewables in Argentina's energy mix to 20 percent by 2025. The results of a bidding process launched last year for new renewable investments was promising, and a new round is scheduled for May 2017.

Renewable energy in South America is beneficial not only for environmental reasons, but also importantly for energy security and economic growth in the region. Despite the region's rich fossil fuel resources, many South American countries are large energy importers. Chile is one of these countries. As a result of its latest auction of energy contracts, prices in 2025 should be a third lower than they are now, according to my Columbia colleague Andrés Velasco, a former finance minister.[59] Large opportunities exist to reduce energy demand growth in South America through energy pricing reforms, energy efficiency standards, and improved mass transit systems, among other measures.

---

55 Felipe Iturrieta and Alexandra Ulmer, "Chile Rejects HidroAysen, Hydropower Project can Appeal," *Reuters*, June 10, 2014, http://www.reuters.com/article/us-chile-hidroaysen-idUSKBN0EL1WR20140610;
John Vidal, "Major Amazon dam opposed by tribes fails to get environmental licence," *The Guardian*, August 5, 2016, https://www.theguardian.com/environment/2016/aug/05/major-amazon-dam-brazil-opposed-by-tribes-fails-get-environmental-license.

56 "Latin America is set to become a leader in alternative energy," *The Economist*, December 10, 2016, http://www.economist.com/news/americas/21711307-power-andean-sun-latin-america-set-become-leader-alternative-energy.

57 IEA, "Medium-Term Renewable Energy Market Report 2016", *IEA*, p.84.

58 Macquarie Research, "Latin America power market: Should I stay or should I go?," October 5, 2016, p.21.

59 "Latin America is set to become a leader in alternative energy," *The Economist*, December 10, 2016, http://www.economist.com/news/americas/21711307-power-andean-sun-latin-america-set-become-leader-alternative-energy.

Brazil was an early pioneer of biofuel production, and remains the world's largest sugarcane ethanol producer and second largest biofuel producer (after the US) to this day.[60] Brazil's current ethanol mandate stands at 27 percent (and its biofuel mandate for diesel fuel at 7 percent), but thanks to the country's nationwide ethanol infrastructure, biofuel use is even more widespread in the passenger car segment. More than 70 percent of Brazil's passenger car fleet is equipped with ethanol-powered or flex fuel engines,[61] which can run on gasoline, bioethanol, or any combination of the two.[62] In 2013, as many as 94 percent of new passenger vehicle sales were flex fuel vehicles.[63] Biofuels in Brazil accounted for 17 percent of the transport sector's final energy consumption in 2014, compared with 2.8 percent globally.[64]

With the right policies and financing arrangements, South American countries have the potential to lead the clean energy transition and demonstrate that deep decarbonization is not only possible, but also highly compatible with rapid economic development. Costa Rica has an energy policy target to become entirely carbon-neutral by 2021.[65] The country already produces 98 percent of its electricity from renewable sources,[66] and it is currently drawing up plans to electrify much of the country's transportation sector in the next few years.[67] Uruguay plans to achieve carbon neutrality by 2030,[68] and it comes close to Costa Rica in generating more than 90 percent of its electricity from renewable sources today.[69]

Realizing a Clean, Secure and Prosperous Energy Future

As discussed above, South America is rich in energy resources and opportunities—from oil and gas to renewables. While every country faces unique circumstances and challenges, broadly speaking, there are a few common priorities on which South American countries should focus—and on which the US can partner with South American nations to provide support and assistance.

---

60 IEA, "IEA Oil 2017", *IEA*, p.143-144.
61 USDA Foreign Agricultural Service, "Brazil – Biofuels Annual: Annual Report 2016," GAIN Report No. BR16009, August 12, 2016, p.16, https://gain.fas.usda.gov/Recent%20GAIN%20Publications/Biofuels%20Annual_Sao%20Paulo%20ATO_Brazil_8-12-2016.pdf.
62 Francisco Posada and Cristiano Façanha (2015), "Brazil Passenger Vehicle Market Statistics," The International Council on Clean Transportation, October 2015, p.13, http://www.theicct.org/sites/default/files/publications/Brazil%20PV%20Market%20Statistics%20Report.pdf.
63 Ibid., p.4.
64 IEA, "World Energy Outlook 2016", *IEA*, p.550, p.562 and p.622.
65 "Costa Rica pledges carbon neutrality by 2021," *Climate Action UN*, January 20, 2017 http://www.climateactionprogramme.org/news/costa_rica_pledges_carbon_neutrality_by_2021.
66 Kelvin Ross, "Costa Rica Plans to become carbon neutral by 2021," *Power Engineering International*, January 17, 2017, http://www.powerengineeringint.com/articles/2017/01/costa-rica-plans-to-be-carbon-neutral-by-2021.html.
67 David Nield, "Costa Rica went 250 days in 2016 without burning any fossil fuels," *Science Alert*, January 3, 2017, http://www.sciencealert.com/costa-rica-went-250-days-in-2016-without-burning-any-fossil-fuels.
68 Veronica Firme, "Uruguay puts high priority on renewables," *Buenos Aires Herald*, November 21, 2015, http://buenosairesherald.com/article/203404/uruguay-puts-high-priority-on-renewables; Cole Melino, "Uruguay powers nearly 100% of Electricity from Renewables," *Eco Watch*, December 4, 2015, http://www.ecowatch.com/uruguay-powers-nearly-100-of-electricity-from-renewables-1882128501.html.
69 IEA, "Medium-Term Renewable Energy Market Report 2016", *IEA*, p.80.

Economic diversification

While countries like Brazil, Colombia, Argentina and others have the potential to ramp up their hydrocarbon production sharply, bringing in much needed investment and revenue, they should not forget the economic strain of the most recent oil price collapse. The oil industry has long known cycles of boom and bust,[70] and there are good reasons to expect that oil prices, moving forward, may be more volatile than in the past.[71] Even as these countries increase production, they must prioritize efforts toward economic diversification to reduce the government's dependence on oil and gas revenue and better insulate themselves from inevitable price fluctuations in the future. Many Gulf Arab countries, for example, are now undertaking economic reform programs to do just that, catalyzed by the fiscal pressures of the recent oil price collapse.

In addition to diversification, countries also must plan for a rainy day by building up fiscal reserves during boom times. Unfortunately, resource nationalism and mishandling of resource wealth has a long history in many countries across Latin America. The plight of Venezuela should remind current and prospective petrostates of the dangers of the resource curse. Guyana, as just one example, has recently discovered vast hydrocarbon reserves that can transform the country's economy—for better or for worse—and should take note to avoid such pitfalls. The potential for another resource windfall should not induce Argentina to ease off on economic reforms,[72] and Colombia could make its economy more resilient to falling oil revenues with tax reforms, spending cuts and further incentives for foreign investments.

Regulatory reform

There is a long history of countries with large resource endowments setting onerous and aggressive rules for foreign investment, in an effort to capture the bulk of the rents for themselves. While these should understandably be treated as national resources that benefit the nation's people, it is also important for countries not to forget that there is an exceptionally competitive global market to attract capital, technology and investment—and an abundance of opportunities. In order to attract much-needed investment, countries should make their regulatory regimes competitive, transparent, stable and predictable. Brazil's recent efforts to allow foreign ownership and reduce local content requirements are a good example.

Ensuring responsible development

Ensuring responsible development of the region's vast hydrocarbon resources through strong, cost-effective environmental and safety regulations has to be a top priority for governments in South America. This is important not only to protect air and water, public health, and the environment, but also to provide industry with a "social license" to operate and build public trust and confidence that oil and gas production will be done safely. And from the perspective of responsible companies, they

---

70 Robert McNally (2017), *Crude Volatility: The History and the Future of Boom Bust Oil Prices*, Columbia University Press.

71 Jason Bordoff (2016), Congressional Testimony Before the Committee on Energy and Natural Resources, United States Senate, 2nd Session, 114th Congress, April 26, 2016, https://www.energy.senate.gov/public/index.cfm/files/serve?File_id=30FCC68F-7842-4501-85C0-BEC3FF009DFC.

72 "A Century of Decline," *The Economist*, February 17, 2014, http://www.economist.com/news/briefing/21596582-one-hundred-years-ago-argentina-was-future-what-went-wrong-century-decline.

Center on Global Energy Policy

protect against a "race to the bottom," in which competitors profit by engaging in risky or irresponsible practices. That is why, if regulations are well-crafted, with benefits that exceed costs, they are in the industry's best interest.

Nonetheless, energy production remains as controversial in South America, as here at home, especially shale resources in countries like Colombia and Argentina. Specifically, governments across the region need to ensure they have put in place smart regulations so that development is done according to the highest standards of safety and environmental protection. They also need to engage in productive consultations with local communities so that important and real concerns can be addressed. At the same time, they need to enforce existing laws and create a transparent and stable permitting and licensing regime to facilitate industry investment in long-term projects.

Climate action

South America is especially vulnerable to global climate change, given the region's susceptibility to extreme weather events and natural disasters. Earlier this year, Bolivia experienced the longest and deepest drought in the country's history, triggering a state of emergency,[73] protests and rationing of drinking water across major cities for months.[74] Recent floods and destructive mudslides across Peru, Ecuador and Colombia have been attributed to climate change by political leaders in these countries.[75] According to a 2015 study by the Pew Research Center, Latin Americans are the most concerned in the world about climate change.[76]

To address these vulnerabilities, countries across the region need to make sure to build a robust, resilient energy infrastructure that can not only accommodate a very high share of intermittent renewable capacity, but is also resilient to the adverse impacts of climate change. The region should also continue to address the problems of deforestation and land use change-related emissions, which, together, account for two-thirds of Latin America's total greenhouse gas emissions, twice as much as energy consumption.[77]

And South America should continue to engage actively in global climate negotiations. Climate cooperation between the US and Latin America cannot only help make the region more resilient and sustainable, but it can also help us succeed in energy and climate diplomacy. The bilateral climate

[73] Jan Rocha, "Shrinking glaciers cause state-of-emergency drought in Bolivia," *The Guardian*, November 28, 2016, https://www.theguardian.com/environment/2016/nov/28/shrinking-glaciers-state-of-emergency-drought-bolivia.
[74] John Vidal, "As water scarcity deepens across Latin America, political instability grows," *The Guardian*, March 1, 2017, https://www.theguardian.com/global-development-professionals-network/2017/mar/01/water-scarcity-latin-america-political-instability.
[75] Nicholas Casey and Andrea Zarate, "Mud erased a village in Peru, a sign of larger perils in South America," *The New York Times*, April 6, 2017, https://www.nytimes.com/2017/04/06/world/americas/peru-floods-mudslides-south-america.html.
[76] Bruce Stokes, Richard Wike, and Jill Carle, "Global concerns about climate change, Broad support for limiting emissions," *Pew Research Center*, November 5, 2015, http://www.pewglobal.org/2015/11/05/global-concern-about-climate-change-broad-support-for-limiting-emissions/.
[77] Lisa Viscindi and Rebecca O'Connor, "How can Latin America move to low-carbon energy?" *The New York Times*, November 24, 2016, https://www.nytimes.com/2016/11/24/opinion/how-can-latin-america-move-to-low-carbon-energy.html.

agreement between the US and Brazil in 2015, for example, was instrumental to the successful negotiation of the Paris Agreement later that year.[78]

Reforming subsidies and reducing demand

Energy subsidies have been an important driver of fiscal deficits in many Latin American countries in recent years.[79] As noted above, some, like Argentina, have taken steps recently to reform those subsidies. The oil price collapse has provided an especially good opportunity for price reforms, as subsidies can be eased with less of a concomitant increase on consumer fuel spending.[80] Energy subsidies are not only a strain on government finances, but also encourage inefficient consumption, thus reducing resources available for export or increasing imports, as well as increasing greenhouse gas emissions. Further efforts to reform fuel prices can help fiscal balances as well as the environment. While policies are needed to help low-income consumers deal with higher energy prices, a wide body of research and evidence shows that subsidies are regressive and largely benefit wealthier consumers.

Moreover, energy subsidy reform is just one measure to reduce domestic energy demand and greenhouse gas emissions. Policies that boost energy efficiency or encourage mass transit use, for example, could present further economic, energy security and environmental opportunities for South American countries.

Conclusion

South America presents enormous opportunities in energy. But it also faces acute risks that can affect regional stability, global energy markets, and the environment. The US has a strong national interest in helping South America meet its energy development goals safely and responsibly, while together taking more rapid action to address the urgent threats of climate change and the transition to a low-carbon economy.

Continued diplomatic and programmatic engagement between the US government and South American countries is important, through initiatives like the Energy and Climate Partnership of the Americas (EPCA), to help promote open markets, responsible energy development, and action on climate change. Ministers from the ECPA countries—namely all of the countries in the Americas—will gather in Chile on September 7-8, an opportunity for the US to reconfirm its continuing commitment to regional collaboration. This can help ensure that the Americas remains an area of strong and constructive engagement on energy policy, technology, and environmental protection.[81]

---

[78] Office of the Press Secretary, Press Release: "U.S. – Brazil Joint Statement on Climate Change," The White House, June 30, 2015, https://obamawhitehouse.archives.gov/the-press-office/2015/06/30/us-brazil-joint-statement-climate-change.

[79] Gabriela di Bella, et al. "Energy Subsidies in Latin America and the Caribbean: Stocktaking and Policy Challenges," *International Monetary Fund*, February 12, 2015, http://www.imf.org/external/pubs/cat/longres.aspx?sk=42708.0.

[80] Keith Benes et al. (2015), "Low Oil Prices: An Opportunity for Fuel Subsidy Reform," *Center on Global Energy Policy*, October 2015, http://energypolicy.columbia.edu/sites/default/files/energy/Fuel%20Subsidy%20Reform_October%202015.pdf.

[81] For more information on the Energy and Climate Partnership of the Americas (ECPA), see: http://www.ecpamericas.org.

Mr. DUNCAN. I thank the gentleman. I am going to go out of order here. The ranking member has a T&I hearing going on he would like to get over to, so I am going to yield to him right out of the chute and come back to me. So ranking member.

Mr. SIRES. Thank you, Chairman, for your courtesy. Last year, we took a trip to South America and we were in Chile. We saw what they are doing with solar energy which was pretty incredible what we saw. Then we took a trip over to Paraguay and we saw the dam.

What bothers me is that for years we have known that there has been a lot of resources in South America. For example, a couple of years ago we took a trip to Petrobras. How is the scandal that has been going on in Brazil going to impact going forward with this energy giant? And obviously, what is going on in Venezuela is also very troubling. And most troubling for me is that you have Russia and China waiting in the wings to see how we approach our energy situation in South America.

So can anybody talk about that? Especially with the security of China and Russia?

Mr. Pinon?

Mr. PINON. The challenge, I think, like all of us, all three of us here with you, is not in the resource base. In fact, I will even venture to say that the challenge sometimes is not in the fiscal and contractual terms that the host countries put before the international oil companies.

The problem is the lack of continuity and stability in the region. The oil industry sector is an industry in which the capital investment goes up front. I mean when the industry develops a big water project, we are talking about hundreds of millions, if not billions of dollars that are going to be invested in that development period that could be between 5 and 7 years. That is why the industry then needs a return of 25 to 30 years to recover that capital investment. So it is just like if you go to Vegas and all of a sudden you are sitting at a poker table and the dealer in the middle of your hand with a pot decides to change the rules of the game. That is the biggest challenge. That is the challenge in Brazil. That is the challenge in Venezuela. That is the challenge in many of the countries that we, or the industry risks is capital. It is that maturity and political stability and continuity that we need in order to run our business.

By the way, Brazil might very well have a very good end result because I think the situation in Brazil at one time I have gone to the head of the Brazilians and thinking that they were ahead and they were able to do everything themselves. And now they find themselves in a situation that they need outside help, not only from capital investment, but even technology; which, by the way, they are probably one of the best in the world.

The issue of China, for example, one of the things that many people have missed is that in the December concessionary rounds in deep waters of our own Gulf of Mexico or in the Gulf of Mexico by Mexico, the largest winner in the deep waters was China. CNOOC won two blocks right off of south of the U.S. maritime border in the Perdido Fault. So you are going to have China drilling just a few miles from our own maritime border in the U.S. deep water Gulf of Mexico here in the next 2 or 3 years.

So but again, to yield to the rest of the panel, I think the challenge is political continuity and stability that we need in order to run our business.

Ms. VISCIDI. Well, I think in response to the question about Venezuela, it is definitely true that China and Russia are both increasing their stakes. China has been a big investor in Venezuela for many years. Russia has been more recent. They recently—Rosneft recently acquired a bigger stake in an oil project from PDVSA. There is discussion about acquiring other assets from other companies in the country.

The issue is that there is some shortage of cash flow. So I think that both those countries are looking to increase their access to the resources, but they are also pulling back a little bit on the Russian side because of lack of cash, and on the Chinese side, because of concern about throwing more money toward loans that they can't recover, because Venezuela is not able to produce the oil it needs and it is not even meeting the terms of its oil for loan deal with China.

But I think that there is certainly a geopolitical motivation there and it is something that remains, they remain very big players in that country.

I think in terms of Brazil—corruption is a huge problem in all of Latin America. It is becoming clearer and clearer. I think that from the industry's point of view, the corruption scandal is really not, just speaking in kind of technical terms, is not the biggest issue. The real problem for Brazil is that Petrobras has massive debts, limited managerial capability, and had too much responsibility just to manage so many projects and it really needs investment from the private sector.

Mr. SIRES. The two other you would think that they were ahead of everybody else in managing a project.

Ms. VISCIDI. In Brazil?

Mr. SIRES. In Brazil. Can you just talk a little bit before my time is up.

Mr. BORDOFF. Yes, I don't have too much to add. I agree with what has been said. So it certainly is true that Brazil has had onerous regulatory rules like local content requirements and other things and Petrobras is finally crippled by the largest debt burden in the global oil industry.

It is worth nothing that Petrobras' new CEO has developed a strategic plan to restructure the company and reform its policies, deliver more accountability and transparency. And the government has introduced wide-ranging regulatory reforms to attract more foreign investment. So these are promising and they are helping to increase investment, but more certainly needs to be done. I think the U.S. can help with that. And this is important not only for economic development and for the financial stability.

Mr. SIRES. My time is up and I don't want to abuse the privilege that the chairman gave by letting me go first.

Mr. BORDOFF. Okay.

Mr. SIRES. I thank you.

Mr. DUNCAN. I want to thank the ranking member and now recognize myself for 5 minutes.

We talk a lot about quality of life and opportunity for improving the quality of life that electricity brings. And I think we missed that as a talking point, especially on the Republican side, but how electricity can improve the quality of life of so many people—whether that is through just being able to heat and cool their homes, being able to have screens on the windows and windows in the windows that aren't open at night to keep the mosquitos out and cooking food that is fresh from a refrigerator and not worried about spoilage. I mean there is all kinds of things.

So I am not saying that is a huge issue in Latin America, but it is in some areas. I like what I am seeing in Latin America with regard to energy production, energy research, energy exploration. We have seen some tremendous projects such as the solar project I mentioned and the ranking member mentioned in Chile, also the hydroelectric dam that was pretty impressive there. But I also understand the environmentalists don't want to see more hydro in Patagonia and tremendous resource of hydro in Latin America. But then you have got this ecological balance on what you do in pristine areas like Patagonia with energy production. So they are facing their own challenges for energy as well. There is the anti-fracking movement in South America, as well as we see here. So they have some challenges.

Let me ask all of you just a simple question. Is hemispheric wide energy security and independence achievable in your opinion? And I say hemispheric. We have got to think from the Arctic to Antarctic, Canada, Mexico included in this, working with the United States and all of our Latin American friends and neighbors here, is that achievable? Because if it is, to preface the question, if hemispheric energy security and independence is achievable, that changes the dynamics in the Middle East with regard to our dependence on those sources of energy. So is it achievable or not?

Mr. PINON. Yes, it is and the way that we looked at it at the UT is that we divide the Western Hemisphere in five regions. The challenge that we have sometimes is we think that the whole Western Hemisphere can all of a sudden hold hands and sing Kumbaya and that is highly unlikely that it will happen.

What we have done is that we looked at five producing and consuming regions that we think that then there can be a sub-regional cooperation in the Western Hemisphere. The Southern Cone, Argentina, and Chile; Brazil, by itself; the Andean group, Peru, Bolivia, Colombia and Ecuador; what we call the greater Caribbean which is the whole Caribbean region including northern South America; and then North America.

So we from the strategic point of view when you do your long-term strategic work and scenario planning, you have to do it from a regional point of view. But yes, I don't think—it is highly unlikely that the region, the Western Hemisphere as a whole could ever accomplish some sort of strategy in energy. Regionally, yes, we can.

Mr. DUNCAN. Ms. Viscidi.

Ms. VISCIDI. I think that energy security for the region is achievable. I think oil and gas and electricity face very different issues.

Oil and gas is really, particularly oil, but more and more gas or LNG, it is really a global market. It is very fluid. So I think the most important thing is to have open market policies, exports and imports with limited restrictions, so that you can really send oil and gas to the places where it is most needed.

I think in electricity, it is more local. It is harder to transport. So it is more of the issues that you were talking about in terms of opposition to large hydroelectric dams. And I think the solution there is by diversity—portfolio diversity that provides the best energy security and it is more about what reforms need to be made in those countries. But I also think there is an opportunity for electricity integration in some places cross border transmission lines, especially in places like Central America. That can really help a lot to contribute to energy security.

Mr. DUNCAN. Mr. Bordoff.

Mr. BORDOFF. Yes. I agree with that. I think it is possible to have hemispheric security in the sense that the hemisphere produces as much energy as it consumes. I don't know that that necessarily means that we have achieved security and independence because these are globally integrated markets and if there is a problem in the Strait of Hormuz or somewhere else, we are going to see prices at the pump go up because global oil prices will respond regardless of where we get our energy from. And the risks to supply, as we heard with regard to Venezuela, are not only from Middle East or other suppliers, they can be from hemispheric suppliers as well.

So I think security comes from being more open, being more integrated through global markets. If we have a problem with Venezuela and sources of oil supply, we can import crude from somewhere else. If there is a problem with our refineries because of a hurricane or something else, we can bring in product and gasoline and diesel when we need it and that is true for LNG, too. If it makes sense for markets to bring LNG to South America, that is great; but, I think if prices rise again in Asia, and it makes sense for U.S. LNG to head to Asian markets or Eastern European countries to help them diversify away from Russian natural gas, then that makes sense, too.

Achieving energy security is not only about where you get your energy from, but about having a diversity of sources of supply and also reducing your dependence on any one source, so energy demand reduction measures are important, too.

Mr. DUNCAN. I think you are all correct. I look at it like this. You have got in the U.S. and Canada, you have got a lot of oil, like the oil sands or the Bakken, and we have got refinery capacity to handle that type of oil. In Mr. Castro's area in Texas, you have got natural gas, you have got gas pipelines going to Mexico. Those gas pipelines continue to extend down through the isthmus in Central America. You have got Panama's great hub for LNG distribution across Central America and South America. You have got Yoho's district in Florida that wants to be an LNG export terminal hub for the Caribbean and the Caribbean nations and lessen their dependence on PDVSA and Venezuela, in general. But if you take it on a broader sense, Venezuela oil comes back on line, you have a stable government there, their oil and natural gas reserves come on line. That is a game changer for the hemisphere as well.

And some of the things we have talked about—electricity generation of a hydro and solar and other things in Latin America that we are seeing; but also the coal, the natural gas, the oil that is abundant there, whether it is through Petrobras, you know, assuming they get their act together and that comes back around without all the graft and corruption and everything that they are dealing with there: Good public policy with regard to the market solutions that President Macri is bringing in Argentina.

So attracting foreign investment I guess is what I am saying in that regard. I just think that there is a tremendous opportunity for us, if we think hemispherically working together. Then the things in the Middle East, the things that OPEC want to do with the spigot aren't quite as important.

I get what Mr. Bordoff is saying is global supply. Energy, whether it is gas or whether it is oil, is traded globally and demand and supply is dictated by global demands. I get all that. But just trying to think outside of the box, hemispherically, and what we can do to change some paradigms and change some dynamics with regard to the Middle East is important.

We touched on Petrobras. That was another question I had, but I do want to ask about Colombia real quick. So Colombia has in the north, I guess northeast, good oil reserves, but the FARC has been an issue with regard to transporting that oil across the country so that it can either be shipped or refined. They have blown up the pipeline, the major pipeline there a number of times. FARC is not an issue any more, according to the peace agreement.

Is that pipeline still a target for other terrorist organizations within Colombia and does the peace agreement in Colombia play a positive role in energy development in the country of Colombia? And I ask you that because we plan on visiting Colombia and I would love to talk with them about this as well. And in fact, I am seeing the President, President Santos tonight. I would love to have this conversation.

So the FARC agreement, how that may play into energy if one of you want to answer that now. I will just open it to all three of you.

Ms. VISCIDI. I could answer that. Well, I think the peace agreement should help to reduce security problems with the FARC, but the ELN is still—they haven't started negotiations with the ELN. So there is no peace agreement. And the ELN is actually the guerrilla group that is more active in pipeline attacks. So that problem has not gone away as a result of the peace agreement.

I think that the peace agreement isn't just about——

Mr. DUNCAN. It is problematic for Colombia.

Ms. VISCIDI. Yes. So I mean there are many problems. The peace agreement is not going to solve everything overnight, so an issue like that, not to mention the issue of the potential for former guerrillas to go back to illegal activity has happened with prior demobilization. There are a number of continuing challenges. But I think that the vision of the peace agreement isn't just have the FARC return their arms. It is about a broader rural development. It is about getting the state to places in the country that it didn't have a presence before and integrating poor people into the system of the country. And it is not just the direct combatants. There is also a large number of people, militias affiliated that are not necessarily taking up arms. And all those people need to be integrated into society.

And I think some of the issues with energy development are about kind of integrating people into society, getting the social license to operate. The anti-fracking movement, I think, if Colombia tries to develop its shale reserves to a point—it hasn't really done that yet; but, if it does try to, that is going to be a non-starter with the kind of opposition that you have on the ground.

So I think the peace process could help to sort of resolve some of these local conflict issues and play a role.

Mr. DUNCAN. That is a great answer. We will just leave it right there.

Gentlemen, if you want to chime in later, that is fine. I got out of order. I am going to go Mr. DeSantis from Florida next.

Mr. DESANTIS. Well, thank you, Mr. Chairman, and thanks to the witnesses.

Venezuela, it has just been a terrible situation there, we have been concerned about on this committee for a long time. They have the world's largest proven oil reserves, second largest natural gas reserves, and yet, their national oil company is generating negative cash flows, deep in debt. Clearly, there is civil unrest in the country and major crackdown, violation of human rights by the Maduro government.

In order for Venezuela to become a functioning player in the regional and global energy market, do you think that that is possible as long as Maduro's regime is in charge?

Mr. PINON. No. There would have to be a change in the political and economic way that the country has been run for the last 10 years. PDVSA is no longer the state oil company that many of us, by the way, were very proud to say that they were a state oil company, just like Petrobras today.

The challenge with PDVSA, for example, is that it is going to take them anywhere between 3 to 5 years to bring their full potential back again. By the way, we think that Venezuela could probably again bring on stream another 2 million barrels a day, if not 3 million barrels per day in a period of between 3 to 5 years. The bottleneck is not necessarily geology. The bottleneck is the upgrade and capacity to turn that heavy oil of the Orinoco into syn. crude that can then be commercialized.

But Venezuela has a huge potential. I mean you talk about lower oil prices. I mean I think between Brazil and Venezuela, there is probably anywhere between 3 million to 4 million barrels a day of production that could come on stream, again, not overnight, but certainly once you get the right investments and the technology in place. But no, it is going to take a long time for Venezuela to again recover the oil business that we were all very proud of and to have.

Ms. VISCIDI. I would just add, I think that there are things that could be done under the current government. There were a series of concessions made under Maduro a couple of years ago to some of the oil companies and they did help companies like Chevron to make sure that they were actually making money in the company and other oil companies have asked for some of those sort of concessions to be extended to them, lowering royalties rates, giving more operational control to the joint venture partners, because one of the issues is that PDVSA is just not capable of managing the project. And there are a series of other things. So technically——

Mr. DESANTIS. So let me, Mr. Pinon, you were shaking your head about that. You disagree?

Mr. PINON. No. The experience that this administration has had, the Chavez administration for the last 20 years is very clear that their partnership is just based on a one-way solution.

Mr. DESANTIS. Right.

Mr. PINON. When they need you, they will come to you. But as soon as circumstances change, they are not there, not paying their bills. They can certainly go to a Chevron or a Schlumberger or a Halliburton and say yes, please, help us out. But guess what, when the time comes to send a check and pay the bills, the check is not there. So no. My position is that within this administration and this regime and this political astronomic model, the oil industry in Venezuela cannot grow to its full potential.

Mr. DESANTIS. And I agree with that. I mean I think you are exactly right about the potential and you wonder. You almost have to try to mess this up and I think it is just this socialist model is just so flawed that here we are.

Let me ask you about this. There have been reports that the state oil company gave a Russian company a lien on almost 50 percent of Citgo which is the U.S.-based subsidiary in exchange for I think it was a $1½ billion loan. So Citgo has three U.S. refineries, the sixth largest refinery in the U.S.

Now if Venezuela were to default on its debt payments to the Russian outfit, the Russian Government could potentially become the second largest foreign owner of U.S. domestic refinery capacity. And one, is that true; and two, what could the U.S. do to prevent that from happening?

Mr. PINON. I am going to stay out of the legal and financial risk. I will let my partners handle that. But the 700,000 barrels a day that Venezuela imports today of crude oil to the U.S., 27 percent of that goes to Citgo. The rest, by the way, only goes to four other refiners. In fact, of the 700,000 barrels a day that Venezuela imports today, 90 percent is imported by only 5 U.S. refiners. So the risk of losing that supply it can be manageable.

The issue also with Citgo you have to remember, is that we have to keep those refineries running. From a strategic and national security point of view, Citgo has to continue on running. Also remember, that all of Citgo dealers all throughout Florida and everywhere else are individual owners of those service stations. So in other words, those service stations in Florida and the Carolinas and in Georgia that have the Citgo brand do not belong to Venezuela. They belong to individual businessmen out there. So what will their situation be if all of a sudden Citgo disappears? But for the legal and financial ramifications of that, I will——

Mr. DESANTIS. Mr. Bordoff, do you want to——

Mr. BORDOFF. I would just say I think there are risks in terms of physical supply, but like with all foreign investments, we have processes, including CFIUS and others, to review potential cyber issues, surveillance risks, and other things. And I think even what is going on today would make sense for the U.S. Government to look very carefully before ownership of major refining assets in the U.S. was transferred to a Russian state-owned company.

Mr. DESANTIS. Do you think the tools that are available now are sufficient to do that?

Mr. BORDOFF. I don't necessarily know the answer to that and I suspect they are. I think they are strong tools and we have used them in the past, but I can't say that with certainty.

Mr. DESANTIS. Great. I am out of time. I yield back.

Ms. VISCIDI. Can I just say for the record that I was going to agree with Jorge that I don't see those changes happening under the administration.

Mr. DUNCAN. Go to Ms. Norma Torres from California for 5 minutes.

Ms. TORRES. Thank you, Mr. Chairman, and thank you to our witnesses that are here today or I should say guests. I want to once again voice my concern that there isn't anyone here formally representing the administration and it is unfortunate that they are not able to address our concerns or even learn from what we are talking about here.

As you all know, many South American countries have a large indigenous population whose territories can experience environmental impacts from energy development, whether that is oil, coal, palm oil, solar or hydro. Given that indigenous communities in South America are often marginalized and have a very limited political power, many of them don't even speak the language, how can we ensure that these communities have a voice in this process?

Ms. VISCIDI. Well, I think that there are processes in various countries. A lot of them have signed ILO 169 Convention on prior consultation. So there are legal processes in place to discuss energy projects and other types of infrastructure projects with indigenous communities.

I think in many countries, the issue is kind of legal clarity the implementation having enough government resources and staff to actually make sure that they are there doing the dialogue that they need to do in every country, clarifying. The ILO Convention doesn't give indigenous communities the right to veto projects. These are national issues as well as local issues. And so there is a lot of confusion about who really has the right to make the decision. And I think that more could be done to really clarify the process, put more resources toward making sure the process that is on the books legally is actually implemented correctly.

Ms. TORRES. The original people of those communities or of those countries are often relocated, rivers are blocked or they are dammed. So they suffer quite a great deal and they are not being paid for the loss of the resources in many cases. That is a concern that I think that moving forward from our perspective, we need to be more careful on how we are impacting communities for the sake of helping these countries make a little bit of money.

As you know, Venezuela is blessed with vast oil reserves. It should be one of the richest countries in the Western Hemisphere. Instead, it has become one of the poorest countries in the Western Hemisphere. People are dying in Venezuela. They are dying in the streets because of lack of access to medicine and food or simply from voicing their concerns and appealing to their government.

I would like to ask all of you why do you think Venezuela has been so unsuccessful in turning its oil reserves into prosperity for its people? And what can other countries in the region learn from Venezuela's experience. If we are going to invest in a particular region, how can we ensure that the money that we are investing is being used properly and that there is transparency in this process?

Ms. VISCIDI. I think there are lots of reasons why Venezuela— why the industry has done so poorly. I mean most of it has to do with lack of investment, misusing funds, a lot of corruption by people working for PDVSA, basic upkeep like fixing pipelines, fixing refineries. Their refinery utilization is down to 39 percent of its capacity.

A lot of it has to do with misuse of funds, I would say, also, diverting funds to things that have nothing to do with the oil business. You can only do that to such an extent. But I think it is really kind of the political and management issues of the country that led to that and so I guess that is the lesson for other countries is you know, you have to have a sound system of institutions and transparency, a stable government.

Mr. PINON. There is an English word that is called stewardship. And it is one of my favorite English words because it means just that, the management of your patrimony. And what Venezuela has done or the Government of Venezuela has done is that they have thrown that patrimony away. I mean today the risk of PDVSA and the reason they are below 2 million barrels a day is because they decided to basically go after that petty cash box and take all that money out for projects that have never materialized in benefit for the people.

I don't have a problem in building hospitals and schools and roads, but the national oil company which is your petty cash box built that up so you could have more money and more resources for future generations. And they did not. They basically stole and raided that cash flow box, basically to benefit short term just for political gains. That is where their problem is.

Ms. TORRES. Mr. Bordoff, I am sorry, I am out of time.

Mr. BORDOFF. In 10 seconds I would just note that while this is one of the worst examples, it is by no means the only and in energy studies the issue of a resource curse is well documented and well known, resource nationalism's handling of resource wealth. You can go to Nigeria and lots of other places. So it is a really hard and challenging issue to address and I wish there were more exceptions to that rule. There are a couple, but not many. And it is an important lesson for countries like Ghana and others that are going to have new oil resource wealth coming to try to avoid some of those pitfalls.

Mr. DUNCAN. I want to thank the gentlelady for her question about indigenous populations and hope to take a delegation to Peru. When I was down there with Ed Royce, Chairman Royce in 2013, one of the big issues is property rights, especially in the indigenous villages where the chief determines who lives where and who owns the property, but they don't have any property records. Having good property records of deed of ownership and fee simple and what that bundle of rights is, who owns those minerals, those sort of things, play into that. I think that would be, you are traveling with us, I believe, I think that would be a good topic of discussion and I will try to make that happen because it is very informative.

I am going to go now to the gentleman from Florida, Mr. Rooney.

Mr. ROONEY. Thank you, Chairman Duncan. I would like to just make one comment about the question about Venezuela's refineries in relationship with Citgo. As you know, the heavy oil refineries are very limited in what they can do which reduces the risks that we have by Rosneft having the lien on the asset. Fortunately, it would be a whole lot worse than with Baytown Refinery or Exxon or Bayonne, New Jersey instead of Corpus Christi, Lake Charles, but neither here nor there.

With some personal experience in the area, I would take a little issue with Ms. Viscidi's comment that FARC has not been a problem with pipelines, having had them blow up several of mine in Putumayo. And I would like to comment here, I would like to ask—
—

Mr. DUNCAN. Mr. Rooney, could you pull that mic over a little bit? Thank you.

Mr. ROONEY. I would like to ask Mr. Bordoff, he made a couple of very good comments in his statement about both the unconventional resources in Upper Magdalena, Mono Arana Field, and then the business about the FARC, to continue the chairman's question as to the pros and cons of the FARC deal and how it might affect production, particularly in the area I am familiar with down in Putumayo where we have to take our oil over to Ecuador to get it out of there nowadays.

Mr. BORDOFF. So that was for me?

Mr. ROONEY. Yes, the question about the Middle Magdalena unconventional and about the FARC and Putumayo.

Mr. BORDOFF. Enormous resource potential in Colombia and Colombia's gas production has been declining and its import dependence has been rising. So if it can take advantage of those domestic resources, that would make economic and energy security sense.

I think the peace agreement, the widely held, rightly held, has been beneficial to attract foreign investment to make the country more attractive for companies to come in; but, I think I noted in my testimony that FARC and ELN have opposed foreign investment and now will be incorporated into the political process. So one question is sort of how that plays out and whether it has any impact.

Just a week or two ago, President Santos announced one of the largest offshore gas finds in years so that has huge potential and then there are enormous shale resources in Colombia. I have been in Colombia three times in the last 2 years, intense environmental opposition and indigenous people opposition. Shale is very—fracking is very controversial here in the U.S. It is intensely controversial there.

So if they are going to develop that resource, it is going to be difficult, but very important that government and industry work collaboratively to engage with local communities, address their concerns, have a very collaborative process, make sure that they have strong rules for safe and responsible development in place to build public trust and confidence that you can develop shale the right way. And I think we can provide help and technical assistance in that and we can show evidence and historical experience in the U.S. Not that there is zero risk. Of course there is risk when you develop any hydrocarbon resources, but with the right level of government regulation——

Mr. ROONEY. But you know the first two horizontal wells in Colombia, Mono Arana, were done with no environmental damage and no problems at all.

Mr. BORDOFF. I think that was the point I was making, that I think we can demonstrate a long experience now in the U.S., as I was saying not that the risk zero, but with the right regulations, the right practices, if you operate the right way, you can develop shale resources responsibly.

Mr. ROONEY. Can I ask one more question or is my time up? One more. I would like to ask Mr. Pinon about Mexico, because he mentioned it obliquely in your testimony. You know, we have the lifting contracts in Burgos and Perinello and some of them down south in Cantaralls is about empty as a basin. So how do you feel about the potential reforms that President Pena Nieto has been put and the opportunities for private capital to work with Pemex?

Mr. PINON. The results of the first week of December, December 4th concessions were very transparent. When you have BHP paying excess of $600 million for the farm out of Trion, when you have Chevron joint venturing with Pemex in one of the Perdido faults, and when you have companies like China's CNOOC also going after two of the major blocks around Perdido will tell you that the geological potential of Mexico's Gulf of Mexico is huge. We have known that at UT by the way for a long time because of the geological work that we have done in the region.

The issue is going to be what is going to happen with possibly a Lopez Obrador administration coming in 2018. We think that he is probably going to be another Lula, an individual that when he comes into office, we are wondering what is going to happen and he is really going to surprise some of us. Maybe—I am hoping for that to happen because of the potential that Mexico has.

Mr. ROONEY. Yes, we were pretty scared last time when he almost won. Yes, I couldn't agree more.

Ms. VISCIDI. Could I respond to the Colombia question?

Mr. ROONEY. Yes, sure.

Ms. VISCIDI. I think to clarify, the ELN has traditionally been the group more active in pipeline bombings and they are not a signatory to the peace process.

Mr. ROONEY. Right, they haven't been in yet.

Ms. VISCIDI. So they continue to be a threat. That was just my point. And I think also you bring up a really important point about opening up new areas of the country that were off limits because of security reasons, Putumayo, also Arauca on the eastern coast. This is another way that the peace process brings opportunities for energy, developing energy resources.

Mr. ROONEY. Perversely enough, the peace process worked adversely to the producers working down at Putumayo because as they need to show that they were a tough negotiating partner in

Cuba, they doubled down on the poor folks trying to exploit oil in Putumayo. Thank you.

Mr. DUNCAN. I think the gentleman. We will go now to Mr. Espaillat for 5 minutes.

Mr. ESPAILLAT. Thank you, Mr. Chairman. Certainly, I concur with the witnesses and I thank you for your testimony, that the political instability in Latin America and the Caribbean has been a major hurdle for economic development, in general, particularly energy independence, interdependence, and the advancement of even renewable energy in the region. Not since perhaps the Kennedy administration and its Alliance for Progress have we engaged in real proactive work with the region. We sort of like turned our heads, we fell asleep at the wheel. We have this attitude of benign neglect for the region that has allowed for these new scenarios to develop which have contributed to adverse relationships with the United States.

And so for many years we have not engaged that region substantially in practical terms and as a result we saw the development of very adversarial relationships in the region vis-a-vis the United States. And in fact, we saw the Chinese and the Russians, Iran, and even radical groups like Hezbollah establish themselves right in the region because of our benign neglect.

So my question is how do you see the Trump administration's divestment from the State Department and foreign affairs and sort of like a continuation of this very benign neglect attitude contributing to the continual instability of the region as it pertains to energy?

Mr. PINON. In fact, I think all three of us mention it. I think the best test case that we are going to have in the near term is Guyana. And there is a place that we ought to focus on, both diplomatically and with all of the other resources that we have, it is going to be Guyana. Guyana is about to find a major, major offshore discovery. They are going about to monetize it and that country is not ready for it. And if we want to begin from a root position to help other countries survive this curse that they might very well have of finding oil, it is going to be Guyana.

And the role of the State Department is important and the role of the Department of Energy is also very important. So I would encourage this committee really that if you want to have a test case, if you want to have a poster child program for the next 5 to 10 years, I think Guyana would be it. But yes, the involvement with the State Department, the involvement with the Department of Energy and other U.S. Government agencies in development capacity for a lot of these countries is very important.

Ms. VISCIDI. Well, as I said in my opening remarks I think that the energy engagement is extremely important and I think it should be continued. And it is not just the benefits of these specific initiatives such as technical initiatives that might help countries in South America to develop resources or help Central American, Caribbean countries to improve their regulatory frameworks and find diverse supply sources. I think it is part of the bilateral relationship. It is an agenda item with different countries, among several agenda items; and, as long as these countries are interested, which they are, they are asking to work with the U.S., Mexico, in particular, I think that we should continue this area of cooperation. I think it is very important.

Mr. BORDOFF. I would just quickly add, I think everything we have talked about this morning should be a reminder that very sharp cuts to the State Department budget will be self-defeating for U.S. national interests. It is in our interest to collaborate and cooperate with countries in South America and everywhere else and to have energy production, safe and responsible production, stability, political stability, and opportunities for U.S. companies to operate there.

So as one example, the Bureau of Energy and Natural Resources of the State Department I think has done very, very useful work to help countries technically and to partner. When Mexico was opening up its energy sector, and in other ways, both on hydrocarbons and on clean energy sources, it is important to have robust organizations like that within the State Department.

Mr. ESPAILLAT. Just for the record, I think I can say safely, Mr. Chairman, that this committee has a bipartisan position in support of full funding for the State Department and we continue to provide the tools for diplomacy and other efforts to continue to move forward.

One final question, real quickly, these South American partners, these countries have signed on to the Paris Agreement. And there are very deep concerns for the environment in these countries. Brazil continues to be sort of like the lung of the hemisphere. And hydrofracking continues to be a challenge in many of these countries.

How do you see our potential to withdraw or at least distance ourselves from the Paris Agreement to impact the relationships that we have with these 12 independent nations of the region that have signed on to the Paris Agreement?

Mr. BORDOFF. I am glad you raised that. I mentioned climate change a few times in my oral testimony. And I think South America is especially vulnerable to the impacts of global climate change. Public opinion surveys shows it is the region of the world where the public cares most intensely about the problem of climate change and I think that is partly because they are seeing the real world effects of it. Bolivia experienced the longest and deepest drought in history, triggering a state of emergency. We have seen hydropower affected in other places.

I think it is most likely that U.S. domestic policy action to address climate change will proceed at a slower pace with this administration than may have otherwise been the case. But having a seat at the table, I think as Secretary Tillerson put it, as part of the Paris Agreement, I think makes good sense for the U.S., both so we continue to be part of this. This process is going to go on a long time and political parties may shift in the future, but also because it does provide continued confidence to other countries to move forward with their own efforts.

Mr. ESPAILLAT. Thank you, Mr. Chairman.

Mr. DUNCAN. I owe you some extra time from a previous committee hearing, so I am always going to be lenient. I want to thank the witnesses. You all have been fabulous. This has been a great topic for us to discuss. It is something that we are going to continue talking about because I think about the United States and Colombia with Plan Colombia and how our countries really became closer over a certain aspect and then led to free trade agreements and so I think energy is a segue to a much stronger relationship with the United States and other Latin American countries, but also all across the hemisphere as a segue to closeness here in this neighborhood, so to speak. So I look forward to discussing these type issues with leaders of the South American, Latin American countries.

And so with that, I will just say that pursuant to Committee Rule 7, members of the subcommittee will be permitted to submit written statements to be included in the official hearing record and without objection, the hearing record will remain open for 5 business days to allow statements, questions, extraneous materials for the record, subject to the length limitation of the rules. There may be additional questions that members may have. They may submit those in writing. I would ask the witnesses to just try to answer those if you can. That is rare, but just due to other hearings around the Hill today, some members may not have been able to make it.

I want to thank you again. I want to thank the committee members for their input and activity here today and with that we will stand adjourned.

[Whereupon, at 11:18 a.m., the subcommittee was adjourned.]

APPENDIX

MATERIAL SUBMITTED FOR THE RECORD

SUBCOMMITTEE HEARING NOTICE
COMMITTEE ON FOREIGN AFFAIRS
U.S. HOUSE OF REPRESENTATIVES
WASHINGTON, DC 20515-6128

Subcommittee on the Western Hemisphere
Jeff Duncan (R-SC), Chairman

TO: MEMBERS OF THE COMMITTEE ON FOREIGN AFFAIRS

You are respectfully requested to attend an OPEN hearing of the Committee on Foreign Affairs, to be held by the Subcommittee on the Western Hemisphere in Room 2172 of the Rayburn House Office Building (and available live on the Committee website at http://www.ForeignAffairs.house.gov):

DATE: Wednesday, May 17, 2017

TIME: 10:00 a.m.

SUBJECT: Energy Opportunities in South America

WITNESSES:

Mr. Jorge R. Pinon
Director
Latin America and Caribbean Program
Jackson School of Geosciences
The University of Texas at Austin

Ms. Lisa Viscidi
Director
Energy, Climate Change, and Extractive Industries Program
Inter-American Dialogue

Mr. Jason Bordoff
Professor and Director
Center on Global Energy Policy
School of International and Public Affairs
Columbia University

By Direction of the Chairman

The Committee on Foreign Affairs seeks to make its facilities accessible to persons with disabilities. If you are in need of special accommodations, please call 202/225-5021 at least four business days in advance of the event, whenever practicable. Questions with regard to special accommodations in general (including availability of Committee materials in alternative formats and assistive listening devices) may be directed to the Committee.

COMMITTEE ON FOREIGN AFFAIRS

MINUTES OF SUBCOMMITTEE ON *the Western Hemisphere* HEARING

Day *Wednesday* Date *May 17, 2017* Room *2172*

Starting Time *10:00 AM* **Ending Time** *11:18 AM*

Recesses *n/a* (__ to __) (__ to __) (__ to __) (__ to __) (__ to __) (__ to __)

Presiding Member(s)

Chairman Jeff Duncan

Check all of the following that apply:

Open Session ☑
Executive (closed) Session ☐
Televised ☑

Electronically Recorded (taped) ☑
Stenographic Record ☑

TITLE OF HEARING:

Energy Opportunities in South America

SUBCOMMITTEE MEMBERS PRESENT:

Chairman Jeff Duncan, Ranking Member Albio Sires, Rep. Mo Brooks, Rep. Ron DeSantis, Rep. Francis Rooney, Rep. Joaquin Castro, Rep. Norma Torres, Rep. Adriano Espaillat

NON-SUBCOMMITTEE MEMBERS PRESENT: *(Mark with an * if they are not members of full committee.)*

n/a

HEARING WITNESSES: Same as meeting notice attached? Yes ☑ **No** ☐
(If "no", please list below and include title, agency, department, or organization.)

STATEMENTS FOR THE RECORD: *(List any statements submitted for the record.)*

n/a

TIME SCHEDULED TO RECONVENE ________
or
TIME ADJOURNED *11:18 AM*

Subcommittee Staff Associate

www.ingramcontent.com/pod-product-compliance
Lightning Source LLC
Chambersburg PA
CBHW081225170526
45165CB00009B/2956
* 9 7 8 1 5 4 8 5 9 9 2 2 5 *